endorsed for
edexcel

Edexcel GCSE

History A: The Making of the Modern World

Unit 3A: War and the transformation of British society c.1903–28

Author:

Nigel Kelly

Series Editors:

Nigel Kelly

Angela Leonard

Updated for the
2013 specifications by:

Jane Shuter

ALWAYS LEARNING

PEARSON

Contents: delivering the Edexcel GCSE History A (The Making of the Modern World) specification Unit 3A

Key terms are emboldened in the text, and can be found in the glossary.

Welcome to the course

Welcome to Modern World History. Studying this subject will help you to understand the world you live in: the events of the last century can help to explain the problems and opportunities that exist in the world today.

How to use this book

There are four units in the course and each is worth 25% of the whole GCSE. This book covers Unit 3A War and the transformation of British society *c.*1903–28. There are four key topics in this unit and you will study *all four*.

- **Key Topic 1:** The Liberals, votes for women and social reform
- **Key Topic 2:** The part played by the British on the Western Front
- **Key Topic 3:** The Home Front and social change
- **Key Topic 4:** Economic and social change 1918–29

Zone in: how to get into the perfect 'zone' for revision.

Planning zone: tips and advice on how to plan revision effectively.

Know zone: the facts you need to know, memory tips and exam-style practice for every section.

Don't panic zone: last-minute revision tips.

Exam zone: what to expect on the exam paper.

Zone out: what happens after the exams.

Top Tips provide handy hints on how to apply what you have learned and how to remember key information and concepts.

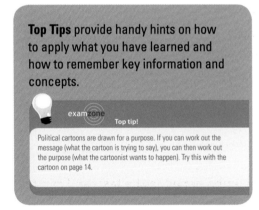

Watch out! These warn you about common mistakes and misconceptions that students often make.

Build better answers give you an opportunity to answer exam-style questions. They include tips for what a basic ■, good ⬤ and excellent △ answer will contain.

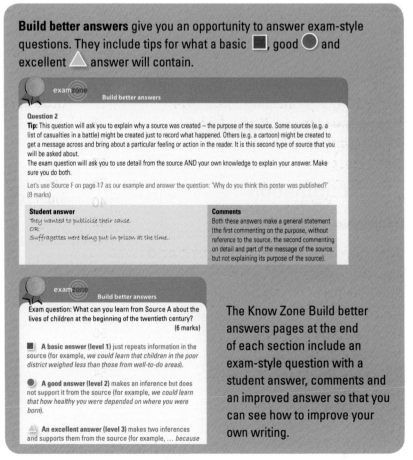

The Know Zone Build better answers pages at the end of each section include an exam-style question with a student answer, comments and an improved answer so that you can see how to improve your own writing.

Unit 3: The source enquiry: an introduction

What is Unit 3 about?

The Unit 3 topics are very different from those in Units 1 and 2. To start with, you are never going to be asked just to recall historical information you have learned. If you find yourself sitting in an examination telling the story of what happened in a particular historical event, you are almost certainly not doing the right thing! Unlike Units 1 and 2, Unit 3 is not about recalling or describing key features. Nor is it about using your knowledge to construct an argument about why things happened – or what the consequences of an action were. Instead, Unit 3 topics are about understanding the importance of sources in the study of history.

History as a subject is not just about learning a series of facts and repeating them in an examination. It is actually a process of enquiry. Historians understand that our historical knowledge comes from evidence from the past ('sources'). Historians have to piece together what has happened in the past from these sources. They need to interpret the sources to build up the historical picture. That is what you will be looking at in Unit 3.

Sources can sometimes be interpreted in a number of ways. They will also have been created for a variety of purposes. This means that historians also have to make judgements about the reliability of sources. You will learn ways of judging whether the information in a source is accurate or not. To make judgements about sources, you need to have some knowledge about the topic the sources relate to. You will need to use this information and the information in the sources to answer many of the questions in the examination. Don't tell the whole story, but select information from your own knowledge to support what you are saying about the source.

The examination

In the examination you will be given a collection of sources to study. Then you will be asked five questions. These five questions will test your understanding of interpreting sources. The good news is that each year the individual questions will always test the same skill. So Question 1 will always be about making an inference. The table at the top of the next page shows how this works.

Question	Marks	Type of question
1	6	Making inferences from sources
2	8	Considering the purpose of a source
3	10	Explaining causation using a source and own knowledge
4	10	Evaluating the reliability of sources
5	16	Evaluating a hypothesis
	3	An additional 3 marks for spelling, punctuation and grammar are available in Question 5.

So before you study the historical topic from which your sources will be drawn, let's make sure you know how to answer each question type. We have picked examples of sources from the General Strike. You won't know the history yet, so you might want to read pages 68–71 before you go any further.

Making inferences from sources

When you read or look at a source and you understand its content, you are 'comprehending' that source. When you make a judgement from what the source says or shows, you are making an inference. Let us look at a source to see what that means.

Source A *A modern historian commenting on events during the General Strike.*

In Glasgow and Doncaster, strikers were arrested, tried and imprisoned. Fear of communism led to the arrest of two men in Wales for possessing communist literature. In Hull, the mayor called out the navy after attacks on trams and serious rioting that seemed to threaten the city. In London, food stocks were moved from the docks to Hyde Park protected by armoured cars.

This is how a historian writing in the late twentieth century wrote about the impact of the strike. In the examination, the sort of question you might be asked would be:

'What can you learn from Source A about the impact of the General Strike?'

You could say: 'In Glasgow and Doncaster strikers were arrested.' That is true, but it doesn't take much working out, does it? It isn't an inference either, because that is exactly what the source says. It is also debatable whether you are talking about the actual impact of the strike.

An inference that is definitely about the strike would be: 'I can learn that the General Strike must have had an impact in different parts of Britain.' Can you see the difference? In the exam you would then want to prove the inference by adding: 'because the source tells me…'.

Considering the purpose of a source

It is important for historians to understand why sources have been created. Sometimes people are just recording what has happened (as in a diary), but sometimes a source is created to get a message across. For example, when a cartoonist sits down with a blank sheet of paper and draws a cartoon, he or she is doing so in order to get a message across. Let's look at an example.

The front page of the TUC newspaper The British Worker *on 5 May 1926.*

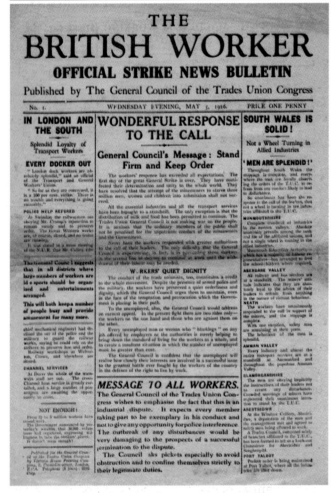

In the examination, the sort of question you might be asked about this source is:

'What was the purpose of this newspaper bulletin?'

You could say: *'because the General Strike was happening'*, but that is a very weak answer. A good answer would look at the detail in the newspaper and work out why those things are being said. The content actually says positive things about the strike ('Wonderful response'). So the TUC wants to show the strike is a success – but for what purpose? The answer is to encourage the workers to continue to strike.

Explaining causation

Question 3 asks you to explain causation using a source and your own knowledge. Read this source.

Part of an interview with a member of the Socialist Party of Great Britain (committed to supporting workers), who took part in the General Strike.

> Ever since the government gave control of industries back to their owners after the war, workers had their wages cut and their working hours increased. There had been strikes before 1925, but it wasn't until the mine owners cut wages and increased hours for the miners AGAIN that the huge wave of support for the miners made a general strike possible. The TUC promised the miners their support, even if it meant calling other industries out on strike. We really felt it was the start of a revolution and the government must have thought so too, for they set up the Samuels Enquiry and gave mine owners a subsidy just to damp things down. But the commission tried to please everyone and pleased no one.

In the examination, the sort of question you might be asked is:

'*Use Source C and your own knowledge to explain why there was a General Strike.*'

Your task is to use the source and your own knowledge to explain why there was a General Strike. You must explain how the source shows this **and** add more from your own knowledge.

From the source you could extract: the post-war treatment of miners and other workers; the TUC promise of support (including striking) to miners; the Samuels Enquiry pleasing no one. You will need to explain how these led to the General Strike, for example the TUC's promise meant if the miners went on strike the TUC would have to call other workers out too.

Now you need to add something from your own knowledge. You could add information about other jobs where wages were cut and work extended (e.g. dockers, railwaymen) or what the Samuels Enquiry said (e.g. wages could be cut, but no increase to the working day).

Evaluating the reliability of sources

Question 4 asks you consider how reliable two sources are as evidence of something. You must refer to both sources and use your own knowledge. Let's look at Source C again. In the examination, the sort of question you might be asked is:

'How reliable is Source C as evidence about how people felt about the General Strike?'

You could say: 'Source C was written by someone who was part of the General Strike.' But this is just a general statement. To produce a good response you need to consider how likely the information is to be reliable, considering what you know about the situation. You also need to ask who has produced the source and why. These things affect reliability. The caption tells you the person interviewed supported the workers, so might have exaggerated support for the miners and how people (and the government) thought the country was close to revolution. It's very important to read the caption carefully and use all of the information it gives about the source.

| **Source D** | *An account of a railway journey during the strike.* |

The train arrived very late and to our surprise we saw that many windows were broken. We were told that we would be travelling by strikers who had stationed themselves near the line. The carriage was raked from end to end with stones and by the time we reached our destination, there was not a window left unbroken on that side of the carriage.

| **Source E** | *A burned-out bus in London during the General Strike. The bus was set alight by the strikers, after the conductor and driver were forced to get off, accused of being strike-breakers.* |

Evaluating a hypothesis

Question 5 asks how far you agree with a statement. You will be expected to use some of the sources and your own knowledge to decide this. This is the sort of question you might be asked:

Source B suggests the General Strike was a real threat to law and order. How far do you agree with this interpretation?

The best answers make a judgement about how far they agree with the statement. They then provide detail from the sources **and** their own knowledge to support this judgement. For example: '…*Source B shows that strikers were being urged to keep order and I know that the first few days were good humoured. However, Source E shows a burned bus. That shows a threat to law and order. Source A tells us people were arrested. It probably depended where you were and when in the strike. …*'

Key Topic 1: The Liberals, votes for women and social reform *c.*1903-14

The early twentieth century saw a significant change in the thinking of the British government. As evidence came to light that huge numbers of people were living in poverty, government thinking began to move away from a belief that people should stand on their own two feet, regardless of what problems they might face. Instead, the Liberal government, which first came to power in 1905, laid the foundations of the modern welfare state with measures to help children, the aged, the unemployed and the sick.

There were changes too in the position of women. The campaigns of the suffragists and suffragettes and the important work done in the First World War all played an important part in helping women gain the vote in general elections in 1918.

In this Key Topic you will study:

- the activities of the women's societies and the reaction of the authorities
- children's welfare measures, old age pensions
- Labour Exchanges 1909, the National Insurance Act 1911.

A woman's place

At the beginning of the twentieth century women did not have the right to vote (**suffrage**) in British general elections. As they could not elect their MP, they had to rely on an all-male parliament to represent their interests as well as to decide on matters of national and international importance.

Most men, and many women, believed that a woman's rightful place was in the home, looking after the children and supporting her husband.

Some people even believed that women were not intelligent enough, or were too emotional, to be involved in such important matters as politics or business. Perhaps a single girl might have a job working as a maid, but married women were not expected to work. In 1911, only 10% of married women were in employment.

But attitudes to women were changing by the beginning of the twentieth century. More girls' schools were opening, women were beginning to go to university and some women were becoming doctors. Women could also vote in local elections, since these were about local matters which might affect the home.

The time had come to push for the right to vote in general elections too.

Source A	*A modern historian commenting on the position of women at the beginning of the twentieth century.*

At this time most people believed in the two 'spheres', a belief that God had ordered that a woman's place was the home, the 'private' sphere. The 'public' sphere, the world of work and politics, belonged to men. Women were called 'angels of the hearth', they looked after their husbands, children and any other family members that needed care.

Source B	*A traditional view of the role of the mother. This painting from 1900 shows the ideal mother looking after her four happy children.*

Activities

1 Read Source A.

   How do you think men at the time would have justified their beliefs?

2 Look at Source B.

   Make a list of all the details in the painting that you think might not be realistic. So why did the artist paint it like this?

The women's societies

Learning objectives

In this chapter you will learn about:
- suffragists and suffragettes
- making inferences from sources.

By the end of the nineteenth century women had begun a campaign to persuade men that they should have the vote. The women who campaigned for the vote became known as **suffragists**.

The National Union of Women's Suffrage Societies (NUWSS)

At this time, the ordinary woman in the street did not have the time or the education to organise political campaigns to win the vote. So the women campaigners were usually middle or upper class. One of these was Millicent Fawcett, who had married Henry Fawcett, a Liberal MP, in 1867. In 1897 she brought the campaigning groups together into the National Union of Women's Suffrage Societies (NUWSS).

This organisation of suffragists was determined to win the vote by peaceful, legal means. The organisation encouraged men to join to help campaign to win over enough MPs to support their cause. These women believed that men were wrong to oppose votes for women and would realise this was so if women put their arguments across in a peaceful and 'sensible' manner.

So the NUWSS trained women to speak at public meetings, produced pamphlets and newspapers and supported candidates in elections who were in favour of women's suffrage. In the 1906 general election, male members of the NUWSS stood against MPs who opposed the vote for women.

The suffragists' campaign was successful in publicising their cause, but some women were angered by the time it was taking to win the argument. They wanted to take more dramatic action to speed things up.

Source A — A poster issued by the National Union of Women's Suffrage Societies in 1909.

Source B — A woman writing in 1851 in favour of women being given the vote.

The real question is whether it is right that one half of the human race should pass through life in a state of forced inferiority to the other half when the only reason that can be given is that men like it.

Activity

You have been asked to take part in a debate about women's rights. The main speaker in the debate intends to base her argument on Source B. You have to tell her why her views are mistaken. What would you say?

Source C *Suffragists at a meeting in 1913.*

The Women's Social and Political Union (WSPU)

In 1903 Mrs Emmeline Pankhurst, a leading member of the Manchester branch of the NUWSS, decided that the time had come to take more extreme action. Together with her daughters Sylvia and Christabel, she founded the Women's Social and Political Union (WSPU). This organisation believed in 'Deeds not Words' and was determined to do anything necessary to publicise the cause.

At first the WSPU was supported by the NUWSS, but the **militant** actions of some of the WSPU members led the NUWSS to withdraw its support. It thought that militant action might put men off, rather than encourage them to support votes for women. It thoroughly disapproved when Sylvia Pankhurst spat at and struck a policeman at a Liberal Party meeting in 1905. The magistrate disapproved too and Sylvia was sent to prison! The *Daily Mail* nicknamed this new militant organisation the '**suffragettes**' and the name stuck.

Not everyone liked the Pankhurst domination of the WSPU, or the increasingly violent WSPU protests. In 1907 some WSPU members broke away to set up the Women's Freedom League (WFL). Its members wanted militant campaigns for women's rights, but did not want to break the law. So from 1903 the women's cause was fought by groups with different views on where to draw the line on militant action.

Source D *The story of the arrest of Emmeline Pankhurst at the House of Commons. It comes from a book written by Sylvia Pankhurst in 1931.*

My mother led a small group to the door of the House of Commons. Here she was handed a note from the Prime Minister stating that he would not see her. 'I am firmly resolved to stand here until I am seen!' she cried. The police inspector began to push her away and his men pushed the other women. To protect her older companions, she struck the inspector lightly on the cheek. 'I know why you did that', he said. She struck him on the other cheek and he called to his men 'Take them in'.

Build better answers

Exam question: What can you learn from Source D about the suffragettes?
(6 marks)

■ **A basic answer (level 1)** just repeats information in the source (for example, *we can see suffragettes would strike police inspectors*).

● **A good answer (level 2)** makes an inference but does not support it from the source (for example, *we can see that suffragettes were determined to succeed*).

▲ **An excellent answer (level 3)** makes two inferences and supports them from the source (for example, *… because this suffragette was quite prepared to be arrested and struck the police inspector twice, and…*).

Militancy and protest

Learning objectives

In this chapter you will learn about:

● suffragette extremism

● evaluating the reliability of sources.

It was not only women who thought that stronger action was needed to publicise their cause. The Liberal prime minister, Henry Campbell-Bannerman, was a supporter of votes for women and he encouraged them 'not to show the virtue of patience, but to go on pestering'.

At first, the suffragettes' campaign consisted of demonstrations and minor acts of public disorder. Sometimes, for example, they would chain themselves to railings outside 10 Downing Street or Buckingham Palace. They hired boats and sailed past the House of Commons disrupting debate through loud hailers. They also attended political meetings to **heckle** anti-suffrage politicians.

In 1908 parliament considered passing a law to give women the vote, but did not do so. In 1911 parliament voted to extend the vote to women, but the measure never passed the Commons and so was not introduced. Prime Minister Asquith instead considered extending the vote to all men (only about 60% of men could vote in 1911) and possibly to women later on. Both suffragettes and suffragists were horrified. The suffragists organised a peaceful 'pilgrimage' from Carlisle to London to show their disapproval. Thousands of supporters joined the march.

The suffragettes reacted in a very different way. They stepped up their campaign, adopting even more aggressive methods. Early in 1912 they started a massive stone-throwing operation in London. At 4pm on 1 March, suffragettes broke hundreds of windows. Police arrested 219 suffragettes, many of whom were sent to prison. They didn't object to being imprisoned. Their court hearings just brought more publicity.

Source A An article in The Standard newspaper, 4 June 1913, describing an attack on a London magistrate by suffragettes in Margate.

'I was walking along, enjoying the breezes on the cliffs,' Sir Henry said, 'when suddenly a woman sprang up from a steep slope, and, seizing me by the leg, sent me staggering backwards. Then another woman tried to push me over the cliff – a sheer drop of around 30 yards. It was very good luck, however, that I swung round and dropped on the ground face downwards. I slipped down several yards, and when I managed to climb to the top of the slope again the women had disappeared.'

Source B Emmeline Pankhurst being arrested after causing a disturbance in 1914.

Suffragettes began to slash valuable paintings, dig up golf courses and cricket pitches, set fire to post boxes and cut telegraph wires. More seriously, they put bombs in warehouses and disused churches, and assaulted leading politicians and carried out arson attacks on their homes. MPs were advised to be careful if suspicious parcels arrived at their homes. They might be letter bombs from suffragettes. In 1913 another attempt in parliament to give women the vote failed.

The 'Suffragette Derby' 1913

In June 1913, Emily Davison left her home near Morpeth in Northumberland and travelled to watch the famous horse race the Derby at Epsom, near London. She stood at the rails at a part of the track called Tattenham Corner. As the horses thundered by she ran onto the course and tried to catch hold of one of the horses. She was thrown to the ground and died in hospital from a fractured skull four days later.

Most historians believe that Emily Davison's death was the result of a protest that 'went wrong'. She was probably trying to disrupt the race (it was the king's horse that hit her) and misjudged the speed at which the horses were travelling.

The suffragettes, however, immediately seized on the event as an example of the commitment of their members to the cause. Here was a **martyr** prepared to commit suicide to publicise the injustices faced by women. Her funeral attracted huge crowds and was turned into a suffragette celebration of the life of a martyr. On her headstone in Morpeth churchyard was written 'Deeds not Words'.

Build better answers

Exam question: How reliable are Sources A and B as evidence of the work of suffragettes? Explain your answer using Sources A and B and your own knowledge. (10 marks)

■ **A basic answer (level 1)** considers a source type in general or the amount of detail (for example, *Source A is from a person who was there*).

● **A good answer (level 2)** considers the reliability of the sources' information by referring to their own knowledge OR considers the nature/origin/purpose of the source and how it might affect reliability (for example, *Source A describes suffragettes attacking a magistrate. We know suffragettes attacked politicians and their homes* OR *Source A was written by the man who was attacked. He might have wanted to make the situation sound more dangerous than it was*).

▲ **An excellent answer (level 3)** combines both elements of level 2.

Source C	*An article in* The Times *newspaper, 5 June 1913.*

The Derby of 1913 will long remain memorable in the history of horse racing. The favourite, Craigenour was first past the post by a head and the victory was greeted with enthusiasm by the crowd. Soon, however, the Stewards announced that the winner had been disqualified and the race awarded to the second placed horse.

The desperate act of a woman, who rushed onto the course as the horses swept round Tattenham Corner, will impress the general public more perhaps than the disqualification of the winner.

Source D	*The front cover of the magazine* The Suffragette *in June 1913.*

Activity

Look at Sources A–D. For each source explain which of the following statements best describes that source.

a It definitely makes suffragettes look bad.

b It definitely makes suffragettes look good.

c It possibly makes suffragettes look bad.

d It possibly makes suffragettes look good.

Reactions to suffragettes

Learning objectives

In this chapter you will learn about:
- opposition to the suffragettes
- considering the purpose of a source.

While there was a great deal of sympathy for the women's aim to win the vote, there was also a great deal of opposition. Organisations such as the Men's League for Opposing Women's Suffrage and the National League for Opposing Women's Suffrage were formed to oppose what the suffragists and suffragettes were trying to do. The opposition came not just from men. Some women believed that the campaign for suffrage was in some way contrary to the natural order of things, where men led and women followed. Such women might join organisations like the Women's National Anti-Suffrage League.

Much of the press, too, opposed women's suffrage. Newspapers published 'humorous' cartoons such as Source A and 'witty' letters calling for 'Fair Play for Babies! Infants demand the right to be heard!'

Source B *A comment by a modern writer on the history of women.*

The people who strongly opposed the women's demand for the vote were known as 'Antis'. In 1908 they set up the National League for Opposing Women's Suffrage (NLOWS). They believed that if women became involved in politics they would stop marrying and the British race would die out. They believed that women had smaller brains than men and were therefore less intelligent. They were also too emotional to make a sensible, well thought out political decision.

Source A *A cartoon published in 1913. Its caption read: 'The best way to silence a suffragette or any woman who demands her rights!'*

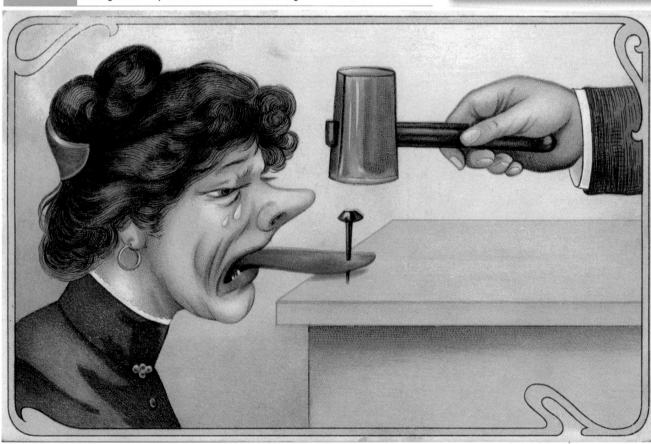

Hunger strikes

But for women, the campaign for suffrage was not humorous; nor was it to the authorities trying to stop the violence. The suffragettes' tactics led to many of them being sent to prison.

Once they were in prison, the suffragettes wanted to continue their protest. Many of them chose to go on hunger strike. They knew that this would cause the government difficulties. If the women were allowed to continue with their hunger strikes, it would lead to death. Many of the suffragettes were from respectable and influential families (Emmeline Pankhurst, for example, was the daughter of a successful businessman and had previously been appointed as a Poor Law Guardian) and their deaths would create serious embarrassment for the government. It could not allow suffragettes to starve themselves to death. Instead it ordered the prisons to force feed them. This involved pushing a tube up the nostril of a hunger striker and down into her stomach. Then liquid food was poured down the tube.

This method was barbaric and, not surprisingly, caused uproar. So in 1913 the government tried another method. Parliament passed the Prisoners (Temporary Discharge for Ill Health) Act. This said that hunger strikers could be released when they became weak. As soon as they regained their strength they were rearrested to finish their sentence.

Soon the act became known as the Cat and Mouse Act. This was because the treatment of the suffragettes reminded people of how a mouse is treated by a cat.

Source C 'The End of the Hunger Strike', a poster from the time of the suffragettes. It is advertising Plasmon Oats.

Women working in a munitions factory during the war.

Source E
A modern historian commenting on the part played by women in the war, from a book written in 2002.

During the First World War the suffrage movements threw all their energy into the war effort. This was recognised by the newspapers and other media who portrayed them in a positive light. It is likely that this had an effect on attitudes towards women and the vote.

Suffragettes and the war

By 1914, opinion was sharply divided about the issue of women's suffrage. Some people thought it was only morally right that women should have the vote. Others said that the suffragettes were just showing that women were irresponsible and the government should not give in to violence. When war broke out the suffragettes called off their campaign and the government released those suffragettes in prison. Instead they campaigned for 'women's right to serve' in voluntary work, factories, agriculture and transport, or even as nurses or ambulance drivers at the front. You can read about this work in more detail on pages 54–57. Such was the effort that women made during the war that Prime Minister Asquith, who had opposed women's suffrage, said in 1917 'I find it impossible to withhold from women the power and right of making their voices heard.'

In 1918 the Representation of the People Act gave women aged over 30 the right to vote. They could also become MPs. In 1928 women were given the same voting rights as men (i.e. all women aged 21 or over could vote).

So was it the suffragists, the suffragettes or the war work which won women the vote?

Source F
A suffragette poster from 1913.

examzone
Build better answers

Exam question: Study Source F. What was the purpose of this representation? Use details from the poster and your own knowledge to explain the answer. (8 marks)

■ **A basic answer (level 1)** makes a valid comment about purpose without using detail in the source for support OR discusses valid detail in the source without linking it to the purpose of the source.

● **A good answer (level 2)** considers the purpose of the source, referring to detail in the source, own knowledge or, for a more complete level 2 answer, both.

▲ **An excellent answer (level 3)** analyses the treatment or the selection of content of the source to explain how the source was used to achieve its purpose, referring to detail in the source, own knowledge or, for a more complete level 3 answer, both (for example, … *a suffragette poster against the Cat and Mouse Act (used by the government against suffragettes on hunger strike, releasing then re-arresting them). The cat is shown as big and fierce with sharp teeth. The suffragette is represented as small and defenceless like a mouse, to get sympathy).*

examzone
Top tip!

Political cartoons are drawn for a purpose. If you can work out the message (what the cartoon is trying to say), you can then work out the purpose (what the cartoonist wants to happen). Try this with the cartoon on page 14 (Source A).

Activity

With a partner, explain whether you agree or disagree with the following statements. Then give each statement a mark out of 10 to show how much you agree or disagree with it. A mark of 10 is total agreement; a mark of 0 is total disagreement.

a Suffragists were too soft.

b Suffragettes did more harm than good.

c The Cat and Mouse Act was a stupid name.

d People would have been offended by the message in Source F.

e Some things are too important to joke about. Women's rights is one of those things.

The state of the nation, 1906

Learning objectives

In this chapter you will learn about:
- rich and poor
- explaining causation using a source and own knowledge.

In the general election of 1906, the Liberal Party won a **landslide** victory. The new government was determined to make changes which would help bring about improvements in the living and working conditions of the people.

At the beginning of the twentieth century Britain was one of the wealthiest countries in the world. Many people had a high standard of living, with comfortable accommodation and good food. More than a million people had an income of at least £750 a year (a very high figure in 1900). But the majority were not so lucky. There was no **welfare state** and their lives were far from comfortable.

Source A	*A scene from a family home in 1912.*

The poor

Recent surveys had shown that much of Britain's population lived in appalling conditions. Seebohm Rowntree found that 43% of York's population lived below the **poverty line**, which he set at an income of around £1 a week for a family of five (the average family size at the time). That meant that they did not have enough money to buy proper food, shelter and clothing.

In 1902 Charles Booth published the results of a huge survey carried out across London. He discovered that almost a third of Londoners were living below the poverty line and that there was a link between poverty and early death. He showed that most people could cope if they were healthy and in work, but once they suffered illness or unemployment families fell into severe poverty – and often ended up in the **workhouse**. These workhouses were set up around the country to give help to those most in need. Conditions were so hard that only the most desperate would want to enter them. Food and clothing were very basic, families were split up and work was long and highly tedious.

It wasn't only Rowntree and Booth who provided evidence of poverty. When the government had called for volunteers to fight in the Boer War in 1899, 40% of recruits were unfit for military service. A royal commission set up in 1905 showed similar results.

So the Liberal government decided to take steps to help the young, the elderly, the sick and the unemployed.

Source B *A family gathering for Christmas tea in 1914.*

Source C *The famous actor Charlie Chaplin talking about life in the workhouse c.1900.*

When we entered the workhouse, my mother was shown to the women's ward. My brother and I went in another direction to the children's ward. Once a week we were allowed to meet. How well I remember the first time we met and the shock of seeing my mother in workhouse clothes. She looked so embarrassed. In a week she had aged and grown thin.

Source D *Comments of an American visiting England in 1909.*

Poor, stunted, bad complexions and badly dressed. That's what these pork-eating, gin-drinking residents of the East End of London are like. I have seen crowds in America, Mexico and most of the great cities of Europe, but nowhere is there such pinching poverty, so many undersized and revoltingly diseased people and such human rottenness as here.

Activities

1 Sources A and B come from roughly the same time. How do you explain the difference between them?

2 What do you consider to be the most surprising fact on these two pages? Explain why you made that choice.

examzone

Build better answers

Exam question: Use Source D and your own knowledge to explain why the Liberal government passed welfare laws. **(10 marks)**

■ **A basic answer (level 1)** generalises without support from source detail or own knowledge.

● **A good answer (level 2)** uses evidence from the source and/or own knowledge to support a reason.

▲ **An excellent answer (level 3)** uses evidence from the source and precise own knowledge to support a reason (for example, … *D says people were undersized and had lots of diseases and we know that there was a lot of poverty because of the Rowntree and Booth surveys which showed the government how bad things were for the poor …*).

Only answers that use own knowledge can reach this level.

Helping the young

Learning objectives

In this chapter you will learn about:
- measures to help children
- making inferences from sources.

The new Liberal government was particularly keen to ensure that the children of the poor were looked after properly. Although a law had made education compulsory for all children in 1880, there were many children who did not attend school, so that they could work and earn a wage for the family – or who were forced to work outside school hours. Children were often poorly fed and clothed. Plus their parents could not afford proper medical treatment.

So the government introduced a series of measures to help children.

School meals

Many teachers were shocked that a large number of children were too hungry to learn properly. Some local charities were providing free meals for children, but this was not enough. In 1906 the School Meals Act told local authorities to provide free meals for their poorest children. By 1914 150,000 children were receiving these meals. However, only about a half of local authorities set up the free meals service.

Medicals

In 1907 the government introduced the school medical service. It told local authorities that all children were to be inspected by a doctor or nurse at least once a year. At first, any treatment needed had to be paid for, but from 1912 this was provided free as well.

Source A | *A letter to the* Yorkshire Post*, 1903.*

I have examined 100 children in Leeds aged 10, 11 or 12. Fifty were taken from a poor district of the city and fifty from a 'well-to-do' district. These were the results:

- 30 of the children from the poor district had rickets, but only 10 from the well-to-do
- 27 from the poor district had bad teeth and 22 in the well-to-do district.

The children in the poor district weighed on average 9 pounds less than those from the well-to-do district.

The children from the poor district were on average 6 inches shorter than those from the well-to-do district.

examzone
Build better answers

Exam question: What can you learn from Source A about the lives of children at the beginning of the twentieth century?
(6 marks)

■ **A basic answer (level 1)** just repeats information in the source (for example, *we could learn that children in the poor district weighed less than those from well-to-do areas*).

● **A good answer (level 2)** makes an inference but does not support it from the source (for example, *we could learn that how healthy you were depended on where you were born*).

▲ **An excellent answer (level 3)** makes two inferences and supports them from the source (for example, *... because if you were from a poor area you were more likely to have rickets and bad teeth and would be shorter and weigh less, and...*).

Source B *A letter written by an official of the Blackburn Board of Education in 1903.*

In Blackburn, though the general death rate has declined significantly over the past 20 years, infant deaths in the city have actually increased. It is also true that many children who survive early infancy are often feeble or impaired in some way.

Source C *A child working with her mother assembling matchboxes at home.*

Source D *Children exercising in the playground in 1908. The government encouraged schools to give healthy exercise to children.*

In 1908 a collection of measures was introduced which became known as the 'Children's Charter'.

- It was now illegal to sell alcohol, tobacco or fireworks to children under the age of 16.
- Working hours for children were limited and they were banned from undertaking certain types of unsuitable work.
- The Children and Young Persons Act of 1908 made children 'protected persons'. Parents could be prosecuted if they neglected their children and it was no longer legal to insure a child's life. (Previously there had been examples of claims for insurance after 'suspicious' deaths.)
- **Borstals** were set up to keep young people in custody rather than send them to adult prisons. Young offenders were dealt with in special juvenile courts and a **probation** system was set up for children.
- The government also set up child care committees to give support to families where children were suffering from neglect or poverty.

Activities

Draw a poster celebrating the great things that the Liberals did to improve the lives of children. Decide which you think was the single most important measure and make that the key thing in your poster.

Helping the elderly, the unemployed and the sick

Learning objectives

In this chapter you will learn about:
- the Liberal government's social measures
- evaluating the utility or reliability of sources.

Having become Chancellor of the Exchequer in 1908, Lloyd George introduced the 'People's Budget' in 1909. This controversial budget raised taxes, partly to pay for new measures the Liberal government was going to pass to help the elderly, the sick and the unemployed.

Old age pensions

In the early twentieth century, how to look after yourself in old age was a real worry for most people. Few people could afford to save or take out private pensions, so when they retired they had to rely on charity or the kindness of their family or friends. The final resort was the dreaded workhouse. Lloyd George said he intended to 'lift the shadow of the workhouse from the homes of the poor'.

The Old Age Pensions Act (1908) introduced pensions for people on a low income who were aged over 70. Pensions were on a sliding scale, depending on a person's income, from a maximum of five shillings a week (25p), down to one shilling (5p). Married couples had a maximum of seven shillings and sixpence (37.5p).

These pensions were paid by the government and did not (at first) involve people making a contribution to a fund while they were in work. This was controversial and some objectors claimed the government was going too far. To old people it was an enormous relief. They no longer had to fear being a burden on their children or being sent to the workhouse. The independence they had during their working life could continue into old age.

In the first year of the scheme 650,000 people collected a weekly pension. By 1914 there were almost one million 'pensioners'.

| Source A | A drawing from 1909 showing the introduction of old age pensions for the first time in Britain. |

| Source B | A report in the Norwich Mercury, 9 January 1909. |

Friday was the beginning of a new era for the aged poor of this country, as the first payment of old age pensions was made. In Norwich there were old people waiting for the doors to open at 8 am and by 9 am the first pensioners answered one or two questions, pocketed their money and walked out.

The Labour Exchange Act 1909

The government was concerned that many men were employed in **casual work** and were frequently **laid off**. Then they needed to look for new employment. So in 1909 it set up a scheme of labour exchanges across the country where unemployed people could register and employers could find workers. This was much more efficient than the old system where workers had to go from employer to employer looking for work. By 1914 there were more than 400 labour exchanges around the country and over one million workers registered.

The National Insurance Act 1911

The government wanted to help workers who became sick or unemployed. This was not a new idea and some workers already contributed to 'friendly societies', which helped them when they fell on hard times. What was new was that the government, the employers and the workers would all contribute to a fund to provide help.

Unemployment benefit was provided for workers in trades such as shipbuilding, engineering and building, where occasional unemployment was common. The worker, the employer and the government all contributed and the worker received a 'national insurance stamp' on his card. If he became unemployed he could claim benefit for up to 15 weeks. The income was small, because the government wanted to help, not just encourage people to avoid looking for work.

Sick pay was also provided. There was compulsory illness insurance for all workers who earned more than £3 a week. Each worker had to pay 4d (old pence) a week. The employer added 3d and the government 2d. So the government was able to say that the workers received '9d for 4d'. For this the worker could receive up to 10 shillings (50p) a week for a maximum of 26 weeks. Families also received 30 shillings (£1.50) on the birth of a child.

These reforms were very important. For the first time the government was dealing not just with the effects of poverty, but was trying to help people so that they could avoid falling into poverty in the first place.

Source C	A government report on unemployment published in 1910.

No one but a rascal is permanently without employment, but large numbers live under the threat of periods of unemployment. When there are economic difficulties employers do not make a small cut in hours for a large number of workers. Instead they sack a small number without warning and with no regard to whether they are single or family men. This shatters many households like eggshells.

Source D	A poster showing a working-class woman using the 30 shillings (thirty bob) received after her child's birth to buy drink. It was published by opponents of the Liberal government's reforms.

"WOT I SES IS, LOOK ARTER BRITAIN'S MANHOOD. LLOYD GEORGE'S THIRTY BOB IS WERY USEFUL!"

Activities

1 Do you think Source A is a realistic picture? If not, does it have any place in a school history book? Explain your answer.

2 Old age pensions removed the terrible worries that some old people had. So why did some people oppose them?

Know Zone
Unit 3A - Key Topic 1

In the Unit 3 examination, you will be required to answer five questions, applying your skills of source analysis to six sources on a topic from the Modern World Source Enquiry you have studied.

You have an hour and 15 minutes to answer these questions. Use the number of marks available for each question to help you judge how long to spend on each answer. The timings below give you some thinking time before you start writing. Remember also to leave a few minutes at the end to check your spelling, punctuation and grammar in your answer to Question 5.

Question 1: 10 minutes	Question 4: 12 minutes
Question 2: 12 minutes	Question 5: 20 minutes
Question 3: 12 minutes	

Here, we are going to look at Questions 1 and 2.

examzone
Build better answers

Question 1

Tip: Question 1 will ask you to make an inference from a source and provide evidence from the source to support it. Let's look at an example.

Source A

> The people who strongly opposed the women's demand for the vote were known as 'Antis'. In 1908 they set up the National League for Opposing Women's Suffrage (NLOWS). They believed that if women became involved in politics they would stop marrying and the British race would die out. They believed that women had smaller brains than men and were therefore less intelligent. They were also too emotional to make a sensible, well thought out political decision.

What can you learn from Source A about attitudes to women at the beginning of the twentieth century? (6 marks)

Student answer	Comments
This source tells me that members of the NLOWS believed that 'if women became involved in politics they would stop marrying and the British race would die out'. They must have thought that women really were second-class citizens.	The first part of this answer merely repeats information contained in the source, so it would be marked at level 1. The last sentence does make an inference (a judgement which is not actually stated in the source) when it says that they must have thought that women were second-class citizens. But it does not say what in the source makes it possible to make that inference. So it is an unsupported inference marked at Level 2 rather than Level 3. Let's rewrite the answer with that additional detail.
This source tells me that members of the NLOWS believed that 'if women became involved in politics they would stop marrying and the British race would die out'. They must have thought that women really were second-class citizens. You can tell this because it says women had smaller brains, were emotional and suggests that their role is only to stay at home and have babies. So that proves they thought they were second-class citizens.	An inference made and well supported, so it's a level 3 answer. Another supported inference would have gained higher marks.

Question 2

Tip: This question will ask you to explain why a source was created – the purpose of the source. Some sources (e.g. a list of casualties in a battle) might be created just to record what happened. Others (e.g. a cartoon) might be created to get a message across and bring about a particular feeling or action in the reader. It is this second type of source that you will be asked about.

The exam question will ask you to use detail from the source AND your own knowledge to explain your answer. Make sure you do both.

Let's use Source F on page 17 as our example and answer the question: 'Why do you think this poster was published?' (8 marks)

Student answer	Comments
They wanted to publicise their cause. OR Suffragettes were being put in prison at the time..	Both these answers make a general statement (the first commenting on the purpose, without reference to the source, the second commenting on detail and part of the message of the source, but not explaining its purpose). To improve, the answer needs tying to the question and better detail from the source AND own knowledge are needed.
They wanted to publicise the awfulness of the Cat and Mouse Act and the way it treated suffragettes. The cat is huge and fierce and the suffragette is small, pretty and defenceless. OR Suffragettes were being put in prison at the time and went on hunger strike, so they were force-fed but people protested about this (thanks to a suffragette publicity campaign). So the government started letting them go when they got weak on the strike and then re-arresting them when they were better.	Both these answers give good detail; the first from the source, the second from own knowledge. If you put both together, it would earn a high level 2 mark. However, neither of them has used this information to explain the purpose of the source.
The suffragettes would have published this poster to get sympathy for the suffragettes and to shame the Liberal government (actually named as the villains on the poster). It tries for sympathy by showing the cat as huge and fierce and the suffragette as small and weak and defenceless. The poster is against the Cat and Mouse Act, a law introduced by the Liberal government that allowed them to release suffragettes they had in prison who were on hunger strike when they got too weak. They had been force-feeding, but public outcry stopped this. Then, when the released suffragettes were well enough they could automatically re-arrest them.	This answer discusses the purpose of the source and uses detail from the source and the student's own knowledge to explain it.

Key Topic 2: The part played by the British on the Western Front *c.*1914–18

In August 1914 Europe went to war. Within months the British Expeditionary Force was fighting in France and was soon involved in a stalemate on what became known as the 'Western Front'. The Germans had hoped to win a quick victory, but the failure of the Schlieffen Plan resulted in four years of bitter fighting with terrible casualties in both the Allied and the German armies.

Despite the invention of new weapons, neither side seemed capable of breaking the stalemate. By 1918, however, the German army was too weak to resist any further. When a final, desperate attack on the Allied forces failed, Germany had no choice but to surrender.

In this section you will study:

- the BEF and 1914
- Britain's contribution to the Western Front 1915–17
- the end of the war.

The British Expeditionary Force, 1914

On 3 August 1914 the rivalries between Britain and Germany over trade, colonies and military power finally resulted in war. The British government sent the British Expeditionary Force (BEF), led by General French, to try to stop the German invasion of France through neutral Belgium.

The 70,000-strong force first encountered the advancing German army at Mons in southern Belgium on 22 August. The BEF was heavily outnumbered as the Germans numbered 160,000 men and had twice as many artillery guns as the British. However, the British troops were so efficient at firing their Lee Enfield rifles that their combined speed made the Germans think they were facing machine guns. But the BEF could do no more than hold up the German advance and was then ordered to retreat to the River Marne. The Kaiser had called the BEF a 'contemptible little army'. The German commander at the Battle of Mons later called it an 'incomparable army'.

Source A	A statement allegedly made by the Kaiser about the BEF, though he later denied ever making it.

It is my Royal and Imperial Command that you concentrate your energies for the immediate present upon one single purpose, and that is that you address all your skill and all the valour of my soldiers to exterminate first the treacherous English and walk over General French's contemptible little army.

Activities

1 When we look at Source B, we get a clear picture of the soldiers waiting to move up to the battlefront. Some of them are smiling. Do you think they are happy? Give your reasons.

2 Pick three other adjectives which you think best describe the look of the men in Source B. Explain why you picked those.

Source B	Members of the BEF in France, 1914.

The failure of the Schlieffen Plan

> ## Learning objectives
>
> In this chapter you will learn about:
> - the beginning of the war
> - evaluating the reliability of sources.

The Schlieffen Plan

The BEF had been sent to stop the German invasion of France. That invasion followed a plan laid down by General Alfred von Schlieffen many years earlier. The Germans intended to invade France, not through the heavily fortified Franco-German border, but instead through largely undefended Belgium. German forces would sweep through Belgium, round Paris and then cut off the French capital from the main French forces in the east of the country. At the same time a German force would fight the main French army on the Franco-German border.

However, progress through Belgium was slower than expected and the Germans changed their plan and drove east of Paris to meet the French army marching back to protect Paris. In the Battle of the Marne (5–11 September) the huge German army (over a million men) fought the French army, supported by the BEF, along a front 200 kilometres wide. The exhausted German army finally retreated 60 kilometres to the River Aisne. The great advance had been stopped. The Schlieffen Plan, which relied on defeating the French by capturing Paris before the main French forces could defend it, had failed.

Source A — *A comment on the failure of the Schlieffen Plan by a modern historian.*

> For almost a month the Germans had pushed forward, often marching up to 80 kilometres a day. Now the Germans had to retreat 60 kilometres to the River Aisne. The great advance had been stopped. The German commander, von Moltke, told the Kaiser 'Your Majesty, we have lost the war.'

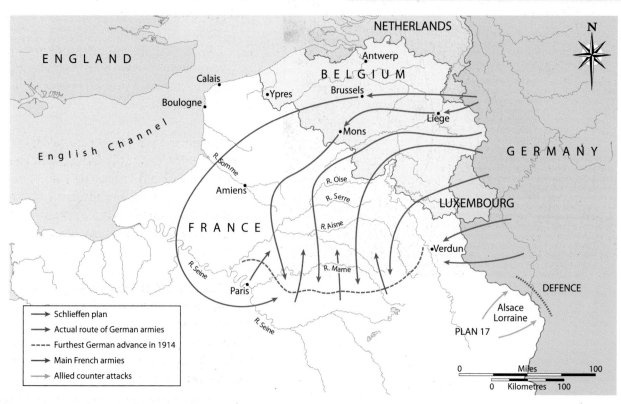

Legend:
- → Schlieffen plan
- → Actual route of German armies
- ---- Furthest German advance in 1914
- → Main French armies
- → Allied counter attacks

Trenches and the race for the sea

After the Battle of the Marne, German troops dug trenches with machine gun posts on top to protect themselves from attack. The French and British also built trenches to make sure that the enemy could not outflank them (go round the side of their defences).

Both sides began extending their trenches sideways. There now followed a 'race to the sea' as both sides dashed north in the hope of breaking through before the enemy had fortified the area. Neither side was able to. In November 1914, there was a fierce battle at Ypres near the Belgian coast as the Germans tried to smash through the French and British defences. They failed and suffered over 134,000 **casualties** in the attempt. The 'winners', Britain and France, suffered 142,000 casualties. It was a sign of things to come.

The failure of the Germans to pierce the Allied defences meant the war quickly became a **stalemate**. Within months a line of heavily fortified German trenches stretched from the Channel coast of Belgium to the mountains in Switzerland. Opposite those trenches was a line of Allied trenches equally strong. This 600-kilometre line of trenches became known as the Western Front. For four years German and Allied forces clashed along this front. Neither side really gained an advantage in that time but millions of soldiers lost their lives trying to.

The Western Front

.... Line of trenches

Activity

How could von Moltke say as early as the second month of the war that the Germans had lost?

examzone

Build better answers

Exam question: How reliable are Sources A and B as evidence of fighting on the Western Front in 1914? Explain your answer using Sources A and B and your own knowledge. (10 marks)

■ **A basic answer (level 1)** considers a source type in general or the amount of detail given (for example, *Source B is a photo; it shows you just what it was like there*).

● **A good answer (level 2)** considers the reliability of the sources' information by referring to own knowledge OR considers the nature/origin/purpose of the source and how it might affect reliability (for example, *Source B looks a bit tidy, it could have been taken to show how organised things were*).

▲ **An excellent answer (level 3)** combines both elements of level 2 (for example, *Source B looks too tidy, maybe it was taken to show good organisation. It only shows part of one trench on a sunny day whilst other photos and writing talk about all the mud. It doesn't show fighting, just roll call*).

| Source B | A British trench. |

Trench warfare

> ## Learning objectives
>
> In this chapter you will learn about:
> - fighting on the Western Front
> - explaining causation using a source and own knowledge.

In 1914 it had been thought that the war would be fought by quick-moving armies and that 'it would be all over by Christmas'. But when 1915 came, millions of soldiers were dug into strong positions facing equally strong enemy positions. The war had ground to a halt – and the generals didn't really know what to do. Britain's secretary of state for war, Lord Kitchener, admitted 'I don't know what is to be done. This isn't war.'

Before the First World War, battles had usually been decided by cavalry charges or infantry troops fighting in hand-to-hand combat. These methods would no longer work. Each side had dug deep trenches protected by sandbags and barbed wire. If one side wanted to attack the other, it had to cross the area between the trenches (No Man's Land). Doing so meant exposing the soldiers to fire from the enemy trench – and huge casualties.

Breakthrough

The generals weren't sure what to do, but they believed that the war could be won on the Western Front. So they poured huge numbers of troops into the area in an attempt to gain the vital breakthrough. But no matter how many soldiers were used, the enemy defences were too strong and the new weapons devised to break those defences not effective enough (see pages 32–35). So no such breakthrough was ever made.

Attrition

Soon, the policy of 'breakthrough' was replaced by one of '**attrition**'. This involved wearing the enemy down so that its supplies of men and equipment were used up before yours. Generals began to calculate whether a battle would bring more losses for the enemy than for their own army. If it did, it was considered to be helping to win the war.

Source A	A German soldier writing home to his family in April 1915.

The battlefield is fearful. One is overcome by a peculiar sour, heavy and penetrating smell of corpses. Men that were killed last October lie half in swamp and half in beet-fields. The legs of an Englishman stick out into a trench, the corpse being built into the parapet; a soldier hangs his rifle on them.

Source B	More casualties: stretcher-bearers bringing in a wounded man over muddy ground at Passchendaele, 1917.

Activities

1 What do you think Lord Kitchener meant when he said 'This isn't war'?

2 How do you explain the extraordinary behaviour of the soldier in Source D?

Verdun

Nowhere was this policy better illustrated than at Verdun in 1916. The German general Falkenhayn knew that the fortress of Verdun was an important symbol of France's military power and that the French would defend it all cost. Indeed, the French prime minister told his generals, 'If you lose Verdun, I will sack the lot of you.'

Falkenhayn talked of how he would cause such casualties that he would 'bleed the French white'.

The German attack began in February 1916 and, as expected, French casualties were very high in defending the fortress. In mid-July the Germans called off their attack as the British had launched the Somme offensive (see pages 36–39). The French had suffered almost 500,000 casualties in that time but the Germans had also lost close to 400,000. Almost a million casualties in a battle which left things much as they were before it had started.

| Source C | *A painting from the time of the war showing a soldier having his wounds dressed during a gas attack.* |

| Source D | *An account of fighting by a soldier on the first day of the Somme offensive. The Somme was a major offensive launched by the British in July 1916. It was a failure with huge casualties in the British forces as they tried to cross No Man's Land. The soldier wrote this account after the war.* |

The two of us dived into a shell hole and began discussing what to do. I came to the conclusion that it would be suicidal to go on and we should stay under cover. However, Lieutenant Wallace said we had our orders and we must go on. At this he stood up and within a few seconds dropped down dead, riddled with bullets. Having observed his actions, I stood up and was immediately hit by two bullets.

examzone

Build better answers

Exam question: Use Source A and your own knowledge to explain why trench warfare was a new kind of war. (10 marks)

■ **A basic answer (level 1)** generalises without support from source detail or own knowledge.

● **A good answer (level 2)** uses evidence from the source and/or own knowledge to support a reason.

▲ **An excellent answer (level 3)** uses evidence from the source and precise own knowledge to support a reason (for example, … *because they were just stuck in these trenches rather than fighting and moving on and the trenches got muddy. It was a victory if you got a few feet of mud or killed more soldiers than the enemy, and because you kept fighting in the same place there were unburied dead bodies everywhere and people just got used to it* …). **Only answers that use own knowledge can reach this level.**

New weapons

> **Learning objectives**
>
> In this chapter you will learn about:
> - attempts to break the **stalemate** on the Western Front
> - evaluating the reliability of sources.

Machine guns

What made attack even more difficult was the development of the machine gun. Although the British were slow to accept the value of the machine gun, the Germans had 12,000 machine guns in 1914 and over 100,000 by the end of the war. The British soon realised their mistake and they too built up their numbers. Machine guns could fire 400–600 bullets a minute and meant that any attack across No Man's Land would be very expensive. What was needed was a way to reduce the effectiveness of the machine gun.

| Source A | British machine gunners in 1916. Notice they are wearing gas masks. |

Gas

In April 1915, the Germans launched a new weapon which seemed to solve the problem. In the Second Battle of Ypres they launched gas shells into the French trenches and killed hundreds of troops. Soon three types of gas were being used.

- Chlorine and phosgene gas caused suffocation.
- Mustard gas ate away the lungs and caused a slow, agonising death.

But soon both sides were using gas and also gas masks to limit its impact. As the war progressed, attacks became less frequent. The horrors of death from gas were recorded by many of the First World War poets. Wilfred Owen in his 'Dulce et Decorum Est' talks about 'an ecstasy of fumbling' as the soldiers rush to fit their gas masks. But one man fails to do so in time and is described as drowning 'as if under a green sea'.

| Source B | A soldier describes the effects of gas in 1915. |

It produces a flooding of the lungs. It is the equivalent to drowning, only on dry land. The effects are these – a splitting headache and a terrific thirst (but to drink water is instant death), a knife-edge pain in the lungs and the coughing up of a greenish froth off the stomach and the lungs, finally resulting in death.

examzone

Watch out!

Remember that if you are asked if a source is reliable you will always be given something to consider what it might be reliable for. Focus on this and remember, 'reliable' means you have to think about whether or not the source is believable, not whether it is useful.

| Source C | A 1918 painting called Gassed. The artist was commissioned to paint this picture as a memorial to those who had died in the war. |

Artillery shells

At the beginning of the war, generals had thought that the most effective weapon would be the artillery gun. These guns varied from small field guns to giant howitzers, which could fire shells into enemy trenches from a distance of 13 kilometres. The British fired over 170 million artillery shells in the four years of the war. An artillery bombardment was supposed to destroy enemy trenches and allow an easy crossing of No Man's Land. Usually what it did was churn up the ground and make No Man's Land harder to cross.

So instead the British developed a system called the '**creeping barrage**'. It involved artillery fire moving forward in stages just ahead of the advancing infantry. When finally developed, the barrage moved forward at 50 metres per minute. The troops followed behind at the same speed. Of course, if the troops and barrage were not co-ordinated properly, the artillery would end up killing its own soldiers. Another problem was summed up best when a British sergeant called the creeping barrage 'One of the most extraordinary advertisements of "look out, we're coming!" I have witnessed in this war.'

Source D *A soldier explains the effects of a German artillery shell on British trenches near Ypres in May 1915.*

Imagine a bright May morning and the platoon busily engaged in washing, cleaning up, cooking and some sleeping. Suddenly, a tremendous explosion, deathly silence and then fearful screams, groans and death gasps. Some of the wounded are shedding blood from gaping wounds and crying in agony – one is asking to be shot. This single shell killed seven men and wounded 18. When the wounded were removed, the trench looked like a room papered in crimson.

Source E *An artillery gun in action.*

34

Tanks

Perhaps the most significant development in the war was the tank. Army leaders at first rejected this new invention as impractical, but when tanks were first used by the British at the Battle of the Somme, in 1916, they terrified the German soldiers.

However, the tanks could only move at walking pace and were very unreliable. Most of the huge machines broke down in the mud. But at Cambrai in 1917 British tanks broke through German trenches and pushed them back nearly eight kilometres. Although by 1918 the Germans had developed armour-piercing bullets which could kill the tank operators, a new weapon had arrived. Tanks were to play a very important part in the Second World War.

Source F A British tank abandoned on the battlefield.

Activities

Write a letter home to the Prime Minister telling him about warfare in the trenches. Begin it:

Dear Prime Minister,

I feel I must write to explain why the stalemate is continuing on the Western Front...

Exam question: How reliable are Sources D and F as evidence of the impact of 'new weapons' on the Western Front? Explain your answer using Source D and F and your own knowledge.

(10 marks)

■ **A basic answer (level 1)** considers a source type in general or the amount of detail given.

● **A good answer (level 2)** considers the reliability of the sources' information by referring to their own knowledge OR considers the nature/origin/purpose of the source and how it might affect reliability.

▲ **An excellent answer (level 3)** combines both elements of level 2 (for example, ... *seems to suggest tanks didn't work well as it's wrecked, whether in fighting or because it toppled over we don't know. We do know tanks scared the enemy when first used, but also that lots of them broke down*).

The Somme

> **Learning objectives**
>
> In this chapter you will learn about:
> - the failure of the British in the Battle of the Somme
> - considering the purpose of a source
> - evaluating a hypothesis.

In July 1916, the British launched a major attack on the German lines along the River Somme. The British commander-in-chief, General Haig, still hoped to make the '**breakthrough**' but most of the generals just hoped to 'kill as many Germans as possible'. Before the attack, there was a seven-day artillery bombardment during which one and a half million shells were fired onto German trenches. Haig said he doubted that 'even a rat' would be alive in the German trenches.

When the shelling stopped, the British climbed out of their trenches and, following instructions, walked slowly across No Man's Land. At first all went well – there was no resistance. But the Germans had been sheltering underground in specially prepared deep dugouts. When the shelling stopped they rushed back to the trenches and set up their machine guns. Had the British hurried they might have captured the German trenches before the enemy was ready to fire. As it was, they walked, and the Germans emerged from their dugouts to find the British troops 'advancing at a steady and easy pace as if expecting to find nothing alive in our trenches'.

The next few hours were among the worst in the history of the British army. German machine gunners killed 20,000 British troops and wounded almost 40,000 others.

Source A	A memorial erected at the Somme in memory of the men of the 36th (Ulster) Division who died during the war. Nine members of the division won the Victoria Cross during the battle.

But the Somme was not just a one-day battle. Haig now switched his thinking from making the great breakthrough to attrition. Although the new tanks had some success in September 1916, at the end of that month the rains fell and the battlefield turned to mud. The battle ended in November 1916. The Germans had lost 500,000 men; the British and French lost 620,000.

Source B	An account of a soldier who fought at the Somme. It was given in a television interview many years later.

He said 'You will find the barbed wire in front of the German trenches blown away.' Blown away! Nothing of the sort! It was as solid as anything. That was the whole trouble. Wrong information!

Source C	British troops leaving the trenches in a scene from the government film The Battle of the Somme.

exam**zone**

Build better answers

Exam question: Study Source C. What was the purpose of this representation? Use detail in the film still and your own knowledge to explain your answer.   (8 marks)

■   **A basic answer (level 1)** makes a valid comment about purpose without using detail in the source for support OR discusses valid detail in the source without linking it to the purpose of the source.

●   **A good answer (level 2)** considers the purpose of the source referring to detail in the source, own knowledge or, for a more complete level 2 answer, both.

▲   **An excellent answer (level 3)** analyses the treatment or the selection of content of the source to explain how the source was used to achieve its purpose, referring to detail in the source, own knowledge or, for a more complete level 3 answer, both.

38

Source D — *A military historian commenting on the plan to cross No Man's Land at a walking pace.*

The need to walk across No Man's Land at a good pace so as to reach the enemy's parapet before he could was not discussed. Each man carried 66lb – over half his body weight which made it difficult to get out of the trench and impossible to move quicker than a slow walk.

Source E — *A British historian writing about events leading up to the Somme.*

When the British press reported a speech by a member of the government requesting workers in munitions factories not to question why the Whitsun Bank Holiday was being suspended, a German army commander commented that it was 'the surest proof that there will be a great British offensive before long'. So the Germans began practising rushing their machine guns from their dugouts to the parapet. Soon they had it perfected to a three-minute drill.

Source F — *Another casualty. This unfortunate soldier died 30 minutes after being carried back to the trenches.*

Source G — *A German machine gunner describes shooting the advancing British soldiers on the first day of the Somme.*

The officers were in front. I noticed one of them walking calmly carrying a stick. When we started firing, we just had to load and reload. They went down in their hundreds. You didn't have to aim, you just fired into them.

examzone
Top tip!

When asked how far you agree with a statement you **must** make a judgement to produce a complete answer. The question is asking you what you think, but it is asking you to make this judgement not by tossing a coin, but by thinking about the sources and what you know about the subject of the statement.

You need to make sure that you support your judgement by producing evidence, from the sources and your own knowledge, to show each side of the argument. You need to use this evidence to explain why you made the judgement you decided on.

examzone
Build better answers

Exam question: Source B suggests the Battle of the Somme was a disaster from day one. How far do you agree with this interpretation? Use Sources B, D and G, your own knowledge and any other sources you find useful to explain the answer. (16 marks)

■ **A basic answer (level 1)** generalises without support from source detail or own knowledge.

● **A good answer (level 2)** makes a judgement, using support from the sources and/or own knowledge. More complete level 2 answers consider evidence for or against the view (for example, *B says the barbed wire wasn't cut, as had been promised and D tells you how hard it was to get out of the trench and do anything but walk slowly. So that was bad organisation from before the battle started*).

▲ **An excellent answer (level 3)** considers how information/representation in the source was used to achieve its purpose, referring to source detail, own knowledge or, for a more complete level 3 answer, both (for example, *… We know that over 20,000 British soldiers were killed in this battle in the first day. That's pretty disastrous. All the sources seem to point to it being a disaster from day one, or even before. So the wire wasn't cut (B), the soldiers were overloaded and it was hard to do anything but walk (D) and they died in their hundreds (G). It seems the Germans worked out when it would happen too (F).*)

39

Activities

1 It seems a very strange reason to have a battle 'just to kill as many Germans as possible'. Why did the British do this?

2 True or false? Here are six statements about the Battle of the Somme. Using the sources and information in this chapter, explain whether you agree with them.

a The Somme was part of the British strategy of attrition.

b The government was happy to tell people the truth about the war.

c There were heavy casualties in the battle.

d The Germans were caught by surprise when the British attacked.

e The British were confident of success.

f The British soldiers had complete faith in their generals.

The end of the war

> ### Learning objectives
>
> In this chapter you will learn about:
> - the failure of Ludendorff's offensive
> - explaining causation using a source and own knowledge.

In April 1917, the USA declared war on Germany, joining the Allies. Germany would lose the war unless it could win it before large numbers of US troops reached the Western Front. On 3 March 1918 Germany made peace with Russia and began to move troops from Russia to the Western Front. On 21 March, Ludendorff (the German Commander-in-Chief) launched the Michael Offensive on the Western Front. Sixty-three German divisions attacked fourteen British divisions along a 90-km front to try and separate the British and French armies and stop them supporting each other. Over 6,000 big guns fired shells and gas. At first, the British fell back, about 40 km west. The people of Paris began to prepare to evacuate. But Ludendorff's army had difficulties with supplies, and 250,000 soldiers had been wounded and killed. The British stopped them about 20 km from the city.

The first German offensive had failed, but they launched further, increasingly desperate, attacks at Lys (April), the Aisne (May), Matz (June) and the Marne (July). By July, 250,000 US troops were arriving at the Western Front each month and the Allies launched a counter-attack. Allied troops recaptured the land taken by the Germans and German troops were in retreat. Ludendorff told the Kaiser 'We have nearly reached the limit of our powers of resistance. The war must be ended.' The Kaiser ignored him. The Allies continued to advance and huge numbers of German soldiers were killed, wounded or taken prisoner in the last few months of the war.

At 11 o'clock on 11 November 1918, the German surrender was signed in a railway carriage in a French forest at Compiègne.

Source A *German prisoners of war, August 1918.*

Source B | The Menin Gate, Ypres. On its walls are the names of almost 55,000 men from the Commonwealth who died in the fighting, but whose bodies were never found.

Source C | *A comment by a British soldier.*

Towards the end of the war we were so fed up, we wouldn't even sing 'God Save the King' on church parade. Never mind the bloody king, we used to say. He was safe enough. It should have been 'God save us.'

Source D | *A letter home from a British soldier describing an attack on the Germans in November 1918, one week before the end of the war.*

This battle is the best I have ever had and I would not have missed it for anything. We were right on top of the Germans before they could get their machine guns to work and a nice few Germans were killed.

Activity

Can you explain why the soldiers in Sources C and D say such different things?

exam**zone**

Top tip!

Question 5 will list several sources to use to make your judgement, then it will add 'and any other sources you may find useful'. Sometimes the other sources in the paper may be useful to you, sometimes not. Don't blindly refer to all the sources on the paper, but do check the other sources to see if they help you.

42

In the Unit 3 examination, you will be required to answer five questions, applying your skills of source analysis to six sources on a topic from the Modern World Source Enquiry you have studied.

You have an hour and 15 minutes to answer these questions. Use the number of marks available for each question to help you judge how long to spend on each answer. The timings below give you some thinking time before you start writing. Remember also to leave a few minutes at the end to check your spelling, punctuation and grammar in your answer to Question 5.

Question 1: 10 minutes   Question 4: 12 minutes
Question 2: 12 minutes   Question 5: 20 minutes
Question 3: 12 minutes

Here, we are going to look at Question 3.

exam zone
Build better answers

Question 3

Tip: Question 3 will ask you to use both a source and your own knowledge to explain why something happened. It is testing your ability to find relevant detail and show, clearly, how it explains something.

In the exam, you cannot reach level 3 unless you use your own knowledge. Level 3 requires you to use your own knowledge very precisely. Don't be vague. Give as much useful detail as you can. 'Many British and French soldiers died in the Battle of the Somme' is vague. 'Hundreds of thousands British and French soldiers died in the Battle of the Somme' is better. 'About 600,000 British and French soldiers died in the Battle of the Somme' is even better.

Let's look at an example.

Use Source F (on page 35) and your own knowledge to explain why the tank failed as a new weapon. (10 marks)

Student answer	Comments
Source F shows a tank lying upside down by the side of a road or path. The path is quite smooth, but the ground beside it has mud and tree stumps.	This answer simply describes the source. It would be a level 1 answer. To move up a level, it would need to say how the source helps you to understand why tanks failed or introduce something relevant from their own knowledge. It would score a very high level 2 mark if it did both these things. Let's re-write the answer to do that.

Source F shows a tank lying abandoned by the side of a smooth road or path. The ground beside it has mud and tree stumps. One reason tanks didn't do well was they needed a fairly level surface to move across - this one might have got caught on the tree stumps, or broken down in the mud (another thing that happened a lot). But if you look at the far side of the tank, part seems to be missing, so this could have damaged beyond repair by enemy fire.

This answer is much better. It uses detail from the source (the mud, the tree stumps and the hole in the far side) and own knowledge about why tanks didn't do well (needed a fairly level surface, prone to breaking down) to address the question. To reach level 3 it would need to develop the argument using precise own knowledge. An answer cannot reach level 3 without using own knowledge.

When tanks first went into battle in 1916 at the Somme they were terrifying. So they didn't entirely fail. But the problem was that they were a new weapon and they had problems that had to be overcome, many of which were overcome by the Second World War.
Source F shows a tank lying abandoned by the side of a smooth road or path. It might be showing several of the reasons tanks failed to work as well as hoped in the war. One reason tanks didn't do well was they needed a fairly level surface to move across - this one might have got caught on the tree stumps. It might also have broken down in the mud, another thing that happened a lot.
But if you look at the far side of the tank, part seems to be missing, so this could have been damaged beyond repair by enemy fire. Tanks were very slow, so if they were out in the open good artillerymen could shoot them fairly easily once they were in range.

This is an excellent answer. It discusses why tanks failed in a way that ties the information in the source and own knowledge together in a balanced analysis.

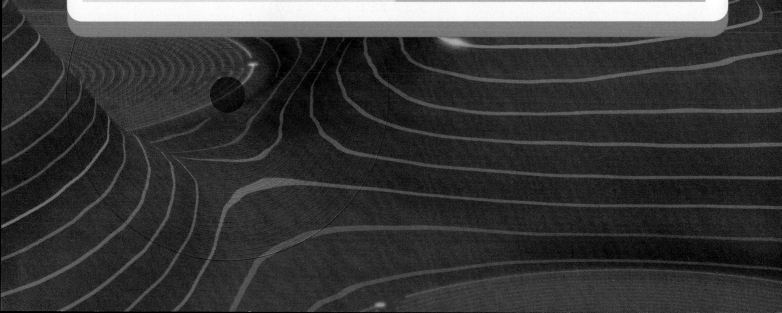

Key Topic 3: The Home Front and social change 1914-18

The First World War was unlike other wars in many ways. It was not only the horrific losses on the battlefield that marked it out as a new kind of war; it was different, too, in the effect that it had on the population at home. Never before had a government passed laws which allowed it to control the news that people heard about a war, allowed it to force men to fight – or face imprisonment, allowed it to control where people worked and even allowed it to water down the beer!

The First World War was fought not just on the battlefield. Such were the demands that were placed on Britain by the fighting that the Home Front was a vital part of the war effort too.

In this section you will study:

- DORA, censorship and propaganda
- recruitment and rationing
- the part played by women.

The Defence of the Realm Act

Learning objectives

In this chapter you will learn about:
- restrictions placed on the civilian population
- making inferences from sources.

The Defence of the Realm Act (DORA) was introduced by the British government in August 1914. This law gave the government far more power than any other British government had ever held before. It was able to **censor** what people heard or read, imprison people without trial, take over economic resources for the war effort and place numerous restrictions on a citizen's life. As the war progressed, DORA was added to and greater restrictions were imposed.

Censorship

The government wanted the people to think that the war was going well. It was essential to keep up morale and this could not have been done if people knew about the terrible losses on the Western Front. So letters from the Front were censored and it was against the law to talk about naval or military matters in a public place. Newspapers were also censored and were told to report only stories of British heroism and German brutality. All news had to be approved by the government press office and official pictures were made available for newspapers to use. (These were often of staged attacks to give the 'correct' impression.)

Free speech also became a victim of DORA. Not only was it illegal to discuss military matters in public, but it was also against the law to make any public comments which might damage morale, spread discontent among workers or harm the government's attempt to recruit soldiers. In October 1915, John Maclean, a well-known Scottish communist, was arrested and charged with uttering statements calculated to 'prejudice recruiting'. He was fined £5 and imprisoned for five days when he refused to pay. He was then dismissed from his post as a teacher.

Source A — *From a book on the First World War written in 1972.*

The philosopher and mathematician Bertrand Russell was fined for issuing a pamphlet protesting at a two-year sentence given to a conscientious objector. He was sacked from his job as a lecturer at Cambridge University and refused a passport to the United States where he had been given a job at Harvard University. Later in the war he was sentenced to six months' imprisonment for publishing a pacifist article.

Source B — *A soldier's letter in 1914 explaining to his son why he was not allowed to give him details of where he was stationed.*

I am not allowed to tell you where I am because the general is afraid you might tell someone at school. He might tell the German master and the German master might telegraph the Kaiser and tell him. Then the Kaiser would send an aeroplane to drop bombs on us.

Controlling industry

The government was also given the power to force people to stay in jobs which were vital to the war effort. Workers were not allowed to transfer to other jobs for better pay if their existing jobs were in key industries, such as munitions. This became even more important when there was a munitions crisis in 1915 as soldiers ran out of artillery shells. Private companies were unable to produce enough munitions. They were struggling to get enough metal, coal, rubber and other materials. So the government took control of co-ordinating the supply of materials. It also set up its own munitions factories and took over the coalmines.

| Source C | A notice banning a meeting in Glasgow in 1917. The Provisional Committee of the Workers' and Soldiers' Council was a communist organisation. |

CITY OF GLASGOW

PROHIBITION OF MEETING

OF

WORKERS' & SOLDIERS' COUNCIL

WE, the undersigned, acting under special authority conferred upon us by the Secretary for Scotland in pursuance of Regulation 9a of the Defence of the Realm Regulations, DO HEREBY PROHIBIT THE HOLDING OF THE MEETING IN GLASGOW, on Saturday, 11th August, 1917, called by the Provisional Committee of the Workers' and Soldiers' Council, in whatever place it may be proposed to hold the same.

THOMAS DUNLOP, Lord Provost.
J. V. STEVENSON, Chief Constable.

Personal restrictions

DORA gave the government the right to introduce food **rationing** (see pages 52–53) and also to control alcohol consumption. Public house opening times were restricted. They were allowed to open only from midday to 2.30 pm and 6.30 pm to 9.30 pm daily. Beer was also watered down. These measures were to control drunkenness and improve productivity. British Summer Time was also introduced to give more daylight hours to work in.

You must not:

- buy binoculars
- melt down gold or silver
- light bonfires or fireworks
- give bread to horses or chickens
- ring church bells
- buy a round of drinks
- keep homing pigeons without a permit.

| Source D | This comment was written in a magazine called The Nation in May 1916. It was complaining about the censorship imposed by DORA. The government used those powers to close the magazine. |

It is a tragedy of the war that the country which went out to defend liberty is losing its own liberties one by one and that the government which began by relying on public opinion as a great help has now come to fear and control it.

Propaganda

The government didn't just use the powers of DORA to force people to do what they wanted. They also used propaganda to persuade people to do this. Propaganda is giving out information, true, false or partially true to make people think and behave in a particular way. Government propaganda showed German soldiers as monsters, to make people want to fight them. It encouraged women to do war work, such as nursing, or join the land army. Propaganda came in several different forms, such as posters, films and pamphlets. Censorship was a form of propaganda, because edited newspapers were giving a government version of events.

Source E	A propaganda poster from 1915, persuading women to encourage their men go to war.

examzone
Top tip!

When asked what they can learn from a source, many students just repeat the information in the source or describe what they can see. Students who do well will make an inference – i.e. a judgement that the source does not make directly. So if you were asked what you could learn about Britain in the First World War from Source A, inferences might be that it was too *tough, controlling, anti-pacifist* etc. To get the highest marks you would then need to support these points with detail from the source.

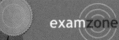

examzone
Build better answers

Exam question: What can you learn from Source D about the Home Front in the First World War?

(6 marks)

■ **A basic answer (level 1)** just repeats information in the source (for example, *the country is losing its liberties*).

● **A good answer (level 2)** makes an inference but does not support it from the source (for example, *there were people who were fed up with the restrictions on personal freedom*).

▲ **An excellent answer (level 3)** makes two inferences and supports them from the source (for example, *… because this magazine is complaining that the government is taking away liberty because it fears public opinion, and…*).

Activities

1 'Putting people in prison for speaking their mind is never acceptable.' Looking at the evidence on these pages, explain whether you agree with this statement.

2 Explain why the government might have forbidden those things listed in the 'Personal restrictions' section.

Recruitment

> **Learning objectives**
>
> In this chapter you will learn about:
> - how the British army was recruited
> - considering the purpose of a source.

At the outbreak of war in 1914 there was a wave of patriotic **fervour** in Britain. Men rushed to the join the army and 'do their bit' for the country. Some were worried that if they didn't join up quickly, they would miss 'the fun'. One Yorkshire cricket team held its Annual General Meeting in September. At the meeting one member proposed that the whole team should sign up for the war. The motion was debated, a vote held and next day the village cricket team turned up at the recruiting office!

Pals battalions

At the start of the war, Britain's army was tiny compared with that of Germany. Lord Kitchener, the secretary of state for war, was put in charge of raising 100,000 volunteers. By the end of September 1914, 175,000 men had volunteered and for the next year over 100,000 volunteered each month. Often men from the same town or organisation were put together in 'Pals battalions'. This clever idea led to towns competing to make sure that they did not look unpatriotic compared with their neighbours. Soon there were Pals battalions from Liverpool, Sheffield, Accrington and many other towns and cities. Often trades battalions were formed, such as the Hull Commercials, the Glasgow Tramworkers – and even the Tyneside Irish.

Men in these battalions trained together and developed close bonds. Unfortunately, no one had realised the downside. On the first day of the Somme, of the 720 Accrington Pals who participated, 584 were killed, wounded or missing. The Leeds Pals lost around 750 of the 900 participants and both the Grimsby Chums and the Sheffield City Battalion lost half of their men. So in some towns and cities there was hardly a street which had not suffered losses. This showed those at home what war was really like.

Source A	A First World War recruitment poster.

Daddy, what did YOU do in the Great War?

The Derby Scheme

The heavy loses in the early years of the war and the realisation that war was not 'fun' meant that by the end of 1915 the army badly needed more men. The government considered conscription (making military service compulsory) and set up a National Register of men aged 15–65. Shortly afterwards it set up the 'Derby Scheme' where men were asked to promise that they would join up if asked. They were told that married men would not be called up before all single men had joined and that those with a good reason not to join up would be exempted. But when less then half of the men in the country agreed to join the scheme, the government was forced to take more drastic action.

The Military Service Acts

In January 1916, the government passed the first Military Service Act. It said all single men aged 18–41 could be called up. A second act in May 1916 extended the scheme to married men in the same age group. 'Doing your bit' was no longer something you volunteered for.

Source B	World War I recruits, 1914.

Source C	A British soldier describes how he signed up in 1914. From A Duration Man: A Staffordshire Soldier in the Great War – Ypres, the Somme and Passchendaele and Italy by Austin J Heraty published by Churnet Valley Books, Dec 1999

'Name, please.'
'Austin J. Heraty, 15 Bailey Street, Newcastle.'
'Age?'
'18, Sir.'
The sergeant looked at me and said, 'Did you say 18, Mr Heraty? I am sorry, but I'll tell you what you can do. You can walk around the town, but if you come back into this room tonight, you must be 19 years of age.' Only then did the penny drop. I walked around the town and in 60 seconds was back in the room. Soon I had signed up.

Activities

1 If you were a man during the First World War how would you feel looking at Source A if:

 a you had joined the army

 b you had not joined the army?

2 Would you agree that this is a 'clever' poster? Explain your answer.

examzone

Build better answers

Exam question: Study Source A. What was the purpose of this representation? Use details from the poster and your own knowledge to explain your answer   (8 marks)

■ **A basic answer (level 1)** makes a valid comment about purpose without using detail in the source for support OR discusses valid detail in the source without linking it to the purpose of the source.

● **A good answer (level 2)** considers the purpose of the source referring to detail in the source, own knowledge or, for a more complete level 2 answer, both.

▲ **An excellent answer (level 3)** considers the treatment or the selection of content of the source to explain how the source was used to achieve its purpose, referring to detail in the source, own knowledge or, for a more complete level 3 answer, both.

Conscientious objectors

Learning objectives

In this chapter you will learn about:
- opposition to conscription
- evaluating the reliability of sources.

The enforced calling up of men under the Military Service Acts was called conscription. For the first time, men had no choice about joining up as long as they passed the medical examination to make sure they were fit to fight. Now, all the men in a family might have to go off to war. A widow in Croydon, London, appealed against the call up of her youngest son (the last of eleven) because the other ten were already fighting. More and more men were taken from jobs and there were no men to do them. The government said that some men were in jobs that were so important to the war (for example train drivers, miners) that they could not be conscripted. As for the other, less 'essential' jobs these were taken over by women who did everything from delivering milk to digging graves in churchyards.

Some men were not exempted, but still refused to join the army. A small group of men refused to fight because it went against their conscience or personal beliefs. These 'conscientious objectors' had formed an organisation called the British Neutrality League to oppose the war. In 1916 they set up the Non-Conscription Fellowship.

Conscientious objectors had to attend tribunals where they faced tough questioning and were often accused of being 'shirkers', 'slackers' or 'cowards'. The **tribunals** had the power to grant unconditional exemption, but usually they allocated the objectors to **non-combatant** duties. Many conscientious objectors performed with great bravery as stretcher-bearers or ambulance drivers. Others contributed to the war effort by giving service at home. It would be a mistake to think of conscientious objectors as cowards.

Absolutists

Most often, tribunals turned down applications completely. So the men were liable for call-up as ordinary soldiers. If they refused to obey the call-up they would be sent to prison. This is what happened to 1500 of Britain's 16,000 conscientious objectors who were **absolutists**. They refused to have anything to do with the war, even in a non-combatant capacity. These 'conshies' (the slang term for conscientious objectors) were sent to prison. Some were even sentenced to death, though had their sentences **commuted** to extensive periods of hard labour, working in places such as quarries.

Source A
An extract from a magazine published by the religious group the Quakers in 1916. The Quakers were pacifists. The article was entitled 'The hardest question of all'.

'Then you are willing to see your country defeated?' That is the question which stops many of us when we are trying to explain our position as conscientious objectors. There is hardly one of us who would say 'yes', but if we say 'no', then back comes the question.
'Then you are willing to let other men fight and die for you, while you stay quietly and safely at home.'

examzone
Top tip!

When they are asked about the reliability of sources, some students assume they can make a judgement by considering source type (for example, *Source B is a photo, it must be reliable*). Good answers consider the nature/origin/purpose of the source and the information it contains. The reliability of Source B for attitudes to conscientious objectors for example needs to consider why it was taken and how representative the women are of all people in the country.

Source B

Women in the East End of London taunt a non-volunteer. One of the women is holding up a white feather. This was given to people who were considered to be cowards.

Source C

A cartoon from the First World War period by Frank Holland, 'An Object Lesson: This Little Pig stayed at Home', depicting a lazy conscientious objector who stayed at home while the rest of his family contributed to the war effort.

Exam-style question

How reliable are Sources A and C as evidence about attitudes to conscientious objectors? Explain your answers using Sources A and C and your own knowledge.

(10 marks)

Activity

If you were a conscientious objector, how would you answer the questions in Source A?

Rationing

Learning objectives

In this chapter you will learn about:

● how the government dealt with food shortages

● explaining causation using a source and own knowledge.

Although most of the fighting in the First World War took place on the Western Front, the 'war at sea' was also important. There were few sea battles between warships (having built very powerful navies, neither Britain nor Germany wanted to risk their battleships). Instead both countries used their navies to **blockade** enemy ports to stop supplies getting through. As an island, Britain had to rely on its merchant sailors to bring food and supplies from abroad. The Germans knew that if their U-boats (submarines) could stop this trade, then Britain could be starved into submission.

The submarine threat

In February 1915, the Germans announced that all **merchant shipping** entering or leaving British waters would be sunk. This was an optimistic statement as there were 15,000 sailings a week to and from British ports and in 1915 the Germans had only 21 U-boats. By 1917, however, the Germans had nearly 200 U-boats and were sinking one in four of the ships bound for British ports. By April 1917, Britain had only six weeks' food supply left and the Secretary of State for War, Lord Derby, admitted that the government was at 'its wit's end as to how to deal with these submarines'. Fortunately, the use of depth charges and the introduction of the convoy system (where merchant ships sailed in **convoy** protected by Royal Naval destroyers) solved the problem. Britain remained short of some foodstuffs throughout the war, however.

Source A *A poster published by the government in 1917.*

Restrictions

The German submarines reduced the amount of food being brought into Britain. As British farmers could not produce enough food for the whole population, there was a shortage and prices went up. In some parts of the country people had to queue to buy goods such as margarine or even potatoes.

Generally, however, it was only from late 1916 that food became scarce. In 1916 white bread was banned because there was a shortage of grain. In 1917, the government asked people to limit their consumption of meat (though the amount allowed was still more than most people could afford to buy). In the same year the royal family announced that it was cutting its food consumption by a quarter. The government hoped that the example set by the royal family would help encourage people to accept restrictions on what they could buy.

The government was keen to avoid the cost and administrative burden of introducing compulsory rationing, but by 1918 it was forced to act. On 1 January, sugar was rationed and by May, margarine, jam, tea and butter had been added. The government also instructed that meat should not be served for breakfast and guests for afternoon tea should be given no more than 42 grams of bread, cake or biscuits. They should also bring their own sugar with them! Ration cards were issued. When people went shopping they had to take these cards with them. Shopkeepers took 'coupons' from customers when rationed goods were sold. This prevented people from buying more than the legal amount of such goods.

Although Britain had come close to running out of food, measures against submarines and the introduction of rationing meant that the threat came to an end. In fact, for many less-well-off people, the regular employment provided by the war meant that they could afford a diet better than the one they had before the war.

Source B *Part of a government report in 1918.*

From London it is officially reported that the percentage of children found in a poorly nourished state is considerably less than half the percentage of 1913. A similar improvement is shown by the figures supplied by Birmingham, Bolton, Bristol, Bradford, Glasgow and Nottingham.

Source C *An extract from the* Observer *newspaper on 8 April 1917.*

At Wrexham a big, fat wagon of potatoes was brought into the town square by farm workers. They started selling the potatoes. The wagon was soon surrounded by hundreds of clamouring families, chiefly women, who scrambled onto the cart in their eagerness to buy. Some women fainted in the struggle and the police were sent for to restore order.

examzone
Build better answers

Exam question: Use Source C and your own knowledge to explain why the government introduced rationing. (10 marks)

■ **A basic answer (level 1)** generalises without support from source detail or own knowledge.

● **A good answer (level 2)** uses evidence from the source and/or own knowledge to support a reason (for example, *C shows the police had to stop a food riot and we know that things were getting scarce*).

▲ **An excellent answer (level 3)** uses evidence from the source and precise own knowledge to support a reason (for example, *C shows the police had to stop a food riot and we know that things were getting scarce. There was a grain shortage in 1916 and propaganda posters were produced to get people to eat less bread. The government wouldn't want people fighting over food, it wouldn't be good for morale, so better to ration it*).

Only answers that use own knowledge can reach this level.

The role of women in the war

Learning objectives

In this chapter you will learn about:

● the significant part played by women in the war

● evaluating a hypothesis.

As you read on pages 9–17, the war had an important impact on the position of women in British society. In 1914 women did not have the vote and many men still believed that women should stay at home and bring up their children, not go out to work.

'Right to Serve'

However, during the war, five million men joined the army and women had to step into their places to keep the country going. Women took on jobs such as bus conductors, drivers or workers on the railways. But attitudes take time to change. Even the government seemed slow to realise how important women were in helping the country fight the war. It took until March 1915 for it to draw up a register of women willing to undertake work. Even then, not all those women were given work. In frustration, the suffragettes organised a demonstration in London in July 1915 demanding the 'Right to Serve'.

Source A *A First World War painting called* For King and Country.

Canaries

The suffragettes' demonstration helped raise awareness of the part women could play, but it was more the increasing demands of war that brought women into work. The losses at the Front and the introduction of conscription meant there was a shortage of male workers.

It has been estimated that Britain was short of 2 million workers once conscription got under way. Employers were very happy to employ women in office jobs, but many of them doubted that women could do a good job in traditional engineering or manufacturing occupations. It was the government that led the way in employing women in such jobs.

There was a need to manufacture supplies for the war, particularly shells for the artillery guns. The government employed large numbers of women to work in munitions factories. In 1914 only 125 women worked at the Woolwich Arsenal; by 1917 there were over 27,000. Munitions work was dangerous and the women's skin was sometimes turned yellow by the chemicals in the explosives (so they were nicknamed 'canaries'). Some factories blew up, killing workers. But the pay was good and some women earned as much as £4 a week compared to the £2 a month they might have earned in domestic service before the war.

The example set by the government encouraged other employers. Women working in munitions factories had shown that with proper training they could do most jobs as well as men. By the end of the war almost 800,000 women worked in engineering jobs.

| Source B | A female coal worker unloads a sack of coal from a van, 28 February 1917. |

 examzone
Watch out!

Source B is a photograph of a woman working in 1917. Students often think that photographs must be reliable because 'the camera never lies'. But this is not true. The camera records what is in front of it, that's all. In exams you should accept that captions tell us the truth and this tells us that she's unloading coal from a van in February 1917. But we don't know how many women did jobs like this, or how long she had been working at this job. She's not very dirty, nor are her clothes, so it was probably a posed photo.

Social attitudes

For many middle-class women, the employment opportunities provided by the war brought them a new independence. For the first time they were financially independent from their husbands. Many working-class women were already used to working, but the wages in the new jobs were often considerably higher than those they had earned before the war. Although women remained very much in the minority in the work force, and were usually paid less than men, the war did bring a significant change in attitudes. Women began to wear more make-up, visit pubs, buy their own drinks and even wear trousers! Although after the war many women lost their jobs when the men returned, a significant step on the road to equality had been taken.

Women in the forces

As the war went on more and more women took on work in industry or joined the Women's Land Army to help grow more food. From 1917 women could work in the armed forces. About 100,000 women joined the Women's Army Auxiliary Corps (WAAC), the Women's Royal Air Force (WRAF) or the Women's Royal Naval Service (WRNS). A further 23,000 served as nurses close to the Front.

Women also played a role in encouraging recruitment. For example, the Mothers' Union took part in a poster campaign to encourage mothers to persuade their sons to join up. Women also gave white feathers to men who had not joined the forces. These feathers were symbols of cowardice.

Source C *A comment by Millicent Fawcett, a leading campaigner for women's rights, writing in 1920.*

> The war revolutionised the position of women. It changed men's minds about the sort of work which everyday women could do. It opened their eyes to the national wastage in condemning women to the sorts of work needing very limited intelligence.

Source D *Percentage of jobs held by women in various areas of employment in Britain 1914–18.*

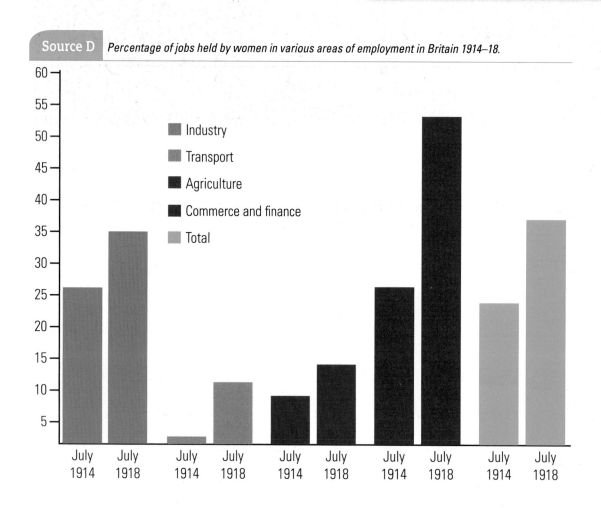

- Industry
- Transport
- Agriculture
- Commerce and finance
- Total

	July 1914	July 1918	July 1914	July 1918	July 1914	July 1918	July 1914	July 1918	July 1914	July 1918

56

Source E — *A comment from a book on Modern World History published in 1996.*

Trade unions resisted the employment of women workers, fearing that women would be paid less and that this would be a threat to men's wages. Most unions did not even accept female members.

Source F — *A comment by a modern historian on the part played by women in the war.*

How could we ever have carried on the war without women? Short of actually bearing arms in the field, there is hardly a service in which women have not been at least as active and efficient as men.

Source G — *Members of the Women's Royal Air Force celebrate the end of the First World War.*

Activities

1 Study Source A. Some people might say that this paints too rosy a picture of what it was like in munitions factories. Write a paragraph explaining why that might be true.

2 Now write a second paragraph explaining why the artist might have done this. Do you think it was just a mistake?

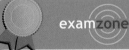

examzone

Build better answers

Exam question: Use Source C and your own knowledge to explain why the war changed attitudes to women. (10 marks)

■ **A basic answer (level 1)** generalises without support from source detail or own knowledge.

● **A good answer (level 2)** uses evidence from the source and/or own knowledge to support a reason (for example, *C says men realised that women were capable of doing jobs that were physically stretching and also mentally difficult*).

▲ **An excellent answer (level 3)** uses evidence from the source and precise own knowledge to support a reason (for example, *C says men realised that women were capable of doing jobs that were physically stretching and also mentally difficult and we know that women's attitudes to their position changed too – they realised it was OK to wear trousers, go to the pub and have a job*).

Only answers that use own knowledge can reach this level.

In the Unit 3 examination, you will be required to answer five questions, applying your skills of source analysis to six sources on a topic from the Modern World Source Enquiry you have studied.

You have an hour and 15 minutes to answer these questions. Use the number of marks available for each question to help you judge how long to spend on each answer. The timings below give you some thinking time before you start writing. Remember also to leave a few minutes at the end to check your spelling, punctuation and grammar in your answer to Question 5.

Question 1:	10 minutes	Question 4:	12 minutes
Question 2:	12 minutes	Question 5:	20 minutes
Question 3:	12 minutes		

Here, we are going to look at Question 4.

examzone
Build better answers

Question 4

Tip: Question 4 will ask you to consider the reliability (accuracy) of two sources for a particular task. You will need to use detail from both of the sources and your own knowledge to answer the question.

In the exam, you have to do two things to reach the top level. You need to evaluate the reliability of both sources by considering the information they provide and weighing in against your own knowledge. You also need to consider the nature/origin/purpose of the sources. Only then, having weighed these up, should you reach your judgement. Let's look at an example.

How reliable are Sources A (on page 54) and D (on page 56) as evidence of the contribution of women during the First World War? Explain your answer using Sources A and D and your own knowledge. (10 marks)

Student answer

Source D is good for their contribution – it shows how the percentage of women working in all sorts of jobs during the war went up between 1914 and 1918, so it is very reliable.

Comments

This answer judges reliability on the amount of detail in the source. It is a good level 1 answer. Other possible level 1 answers are those that judge reliability by source type (for example, *it's a graph, it must be reliable*) or subject (*for example, it's all about women working during the war*).

To reach level 2 the answer would have to EITHER: evaluate the information in the source by testing it against own knowledge for reliability
OR: evaluate the nature/origin/purpose of the source by testing it against own knowledge for reliability.
Let's re-write the answer to do that.

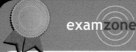

Source A shows women working in a munitions factory. We know women did work in these factories – there are photos like this painting, except the painting shows it as cleaner. But the detail of the machinery and uniforms looks very reliable. It also shows a man, just one, and we know that some men didn't go to war because they weren't fit enough to be in the army or were conscientious objectors and so did war work.

OR

Source D shows how the percentage of women working in industry, transport, agriculture and commerce and finance during the war went up between 1914 and 1918. The caption doesn't tell us who prepared these figures. Was it government propaganda? Was it done by the suffragettes as propaganda? Where did the figures come from? We need to know this before we can say if it is reliable. We also need to know more about Source A for the same reason. It's called 'For King and Country' which sounds very patriotic. It could well have been done as a piece of war propaganda, to get women to work in the factories – we know that they were really dirtier and more dangerous than this one looks.

These answers are much better. They are level 2 answers. They consider the source(s), not just types of source and they also both use own knowledge to support their answer. The key thing is that they explain why they have made their decision. It's OK to say you don't know if a source is reliable – but you have to explain why you don't know.

More complete answers at this level will evaluate both sources, not just one of them. The second answer does this. To reach level 3, an answer would need to do both parts of level 2. Let's do that.

Source A's called 'For King and Country' which sounds very patriotic. It could well have been done as a piece of war propaganda, to get women to work in the factories – we know that they were really dirtier and more dangerous than this one looks (although the detail of the uniforms and what the factory looks like are like descriptions and photos from the time). So we would need to know who painted it and why they did it before we could say it was reliable.

As for Source D, the caption doesn't tell us who prepared these figures. Was it propaganda from the government, or a suffragette society? We need to know where the figures come from before we can say if it is reliable. Having said that, we do know that more and more women were employed in all kinds of jobs; from working as land girls on farms to working in munitions factories, to driving buses. So it's plausible.

This is an excellent answer. It discusses the reliability of both sources in a way that ties the information in the source and own knowledge together in a balanced analysis.

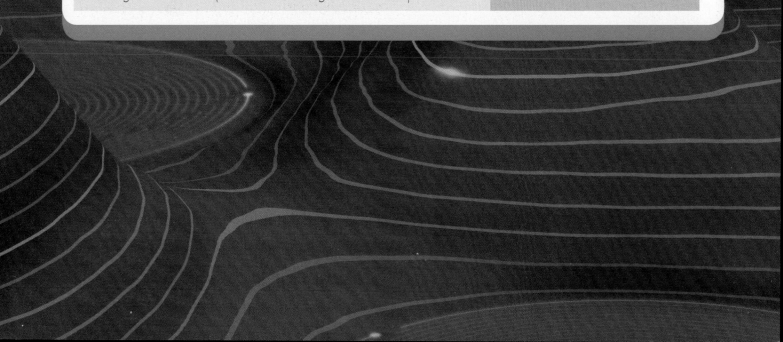

Key Topic 4: Economic and social change 1918-28

The First World War brought a major change in the way people thought about women – and in the work that women did. But once the war ended most people expected women to return to their traditional role as homemakers. Progress had been made in winning the vote but, as women were to find to their cost, the gains they had made elsewhere proved temporary.

This was also a period of considerable unrest in industry. Even before the war, employers had found themselves faced with demands for better conditions and pay. Some of the strikes at that time had political motives as workers tried to undermine the power of the government. Problems continued after the war, particularly in the coal industry. When attempts were made to cut wages and increase hours in the mines, the Trade Union Congress called a 'General Strike'. It failed and union power declined rapidly as a result.

In this section you will study:

◉ the changing role of women 1918–26
◉ industrial unrest 1918–26
◉ the General Strike of 1926.

Equality for women

The First World War had provided women with the opportunity to show men how they could contribute to society. However, after 1918 many of the doors which had opened to them were closed once more.

At the beginning of the twentieth century, Britain was governed by men and largely for men. The 'perfect woman' was a wife and mother who obeyed her husband and looked after their children. A good education was considered to be something necessary only for boys. Wealthy girls were taught how to be 'genteel', but it was thought there was no value in educating working-class girls. The changes brought about by the First World War played a major part in changing some attitudes towards women, but only a minority of men began to see women in a new light and not all women supported the changes that were happening. Many of them enjoyed the role of wife and mother. It is interesting to note that the Women's Institute, which saw women as 'the Housekeeper, the Home-keeper, or better still the Home-maker', saw a huge rise in its membership in the years after the war.

In politics, women had made ground. In 1918 women aged 30 and over received the vote, and in 1928 the Equal Franchise Act said the vote should be extended to all women aged 21 or over. There were now more women voters than men, but women did not play a major part in politics for many years.

Source A *Mother votes in the general election! A photo from 1918.*

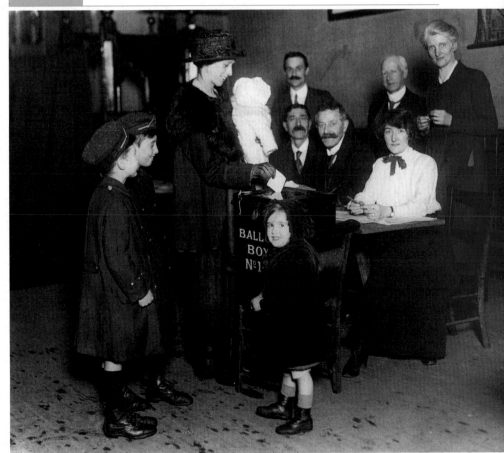

Politics

In 1918 the Parliament (Qualification of Women) Bill was passed allowing women to become MPs. At the 1918 general election, out of a total of 1,623 candidates, only 17 were women. Only one was elected, but she did not take up her seat. Countess Constance Markievicz was married to a Polish count and stood for Sinn Fein in Dublin. She campaigned from Holloway Prison, where she was being held on suspicion of helping the Germans in the war. Even when she was released, like other Sinn Fein members, she refused to take up her seat in protest at Britain's policy in Ireland.

The first three female MPs were all elected in seats previously held by their husbands. Viscountess Astor was elected in a by-election in Plymouth in November 1919 after her husband resigned to become a member of the House of Lords. In 1921 Margaret Wintringham won the seat held by her husband in Louth until his death. In 1923 Mabel Philipson, a well-known musical comedy actress, was elected in Berwick-upon-Tweed after her husband was disqualified because his election agent had spent more than the permitted amount in the previous election. It was not until 1924 that a woman (Margaret Bondfield) became a member of the government.

Work

Once the war finished, most men expected women to give up their jobs and return to their rightful place in the home. So did the government. Munitions workers were paid off with two weeks' extra wages and female civil servants were dismissed. Within eighteen months, three-quarters of the women who had taken on war work had left their jobs. Many of them were happy to give up their work; others were resentful of the fact that they were expected to return to low-paid domestic work and lose the financial independence they had gained during the war. For those who stayed in work, old practices continued. When women married they were often sacked (nurses had to leave when they got married) and women's wages were well below those of men.

> **Exam-style question**
>
> **Study Source B. What was the purpose of this cartoon? Use details from the cartoon and your own knowledge to explain your answer.** (8 marks)

Source B · *A cartoon published by the* Daily Mirror *on 1 March 1924.*

Social attitudes

The belief that women should give up their jobs when they married reflected the continuing belief that men were the decision makers and breadwinners in society. A woman's main task was motherhood, and employment would not allow proper care of the family. Domestic bliss was married life and motherhood. Motherhood without marriage was considered a major indiscretion and unmarried mothers were seen as a disgrace to the family. In 1918, when Marie Stopes published material advocating birth control, she was condemned by the Church and many of the newspapers.

In education, too, things were slow to change. Most girls left school at the age of 14 and less than 1% were educated beyond the age of 18. Oxford University had only 750 places for women and Cambridge did not give degrees to women until 1948.

There were signs of change. From 1923 women could divorce their husbands for **adultery** (men had always been able to divorce wives who committed adultery), but equality was still a long way off.

Source C	Percentage of women in employment in Britain.		
	Single	**Married**	**All women**
1911	70	10	35
1931	71	10	34

Activities

'Source B is not serious as no one could expect babies to vote. Historians, therefore, should take no notice of it.' Do you agree?

Source D	An extract from the newspaper The Morning Post in April 1919.

It has been found necessary to restrict, and in some cases to stop, unemployment benefit to female ex-munitions workers in Sheffield. Three hundred women who have refused to accept work in domestic service have been suspended from all benefit.

Source E	The views of a historian writing in 1996.

In 1914 a woman's place was in the home. Should she need to work, then suitable occupations were decided by men. The First World War was nothing more than a temporary victory. Women had never been welcome in 'men's jobs' and the belief that their presence devalued skills was never overcome. A mixture of threat and incentive ensured that women returned to their 'proper place' and stayed there – until another war demanded their services.

examzone
Build better answers

Exam question: What can you learn from Source E about the position of women in Britain at the end of the First World War? **(6 marks)**

■ **A basic answer (level 1)** just repeats information in the source (for example, *the First World War was nothing more than a temporary victory*).

● **A good answer (level 2)** makes an inference but does not support it from the source (for example, *a woman's position at the end of the war was not much different to what it had been at the beginning*).

▲ **An excellent answer (level 3)** makes two inferences and supports them from the source (for example, ... *we can see this because it says 'a mixture of threat and incentive ensured that women returned to their "proper place"', and...*).

Industrial unrest

> **Learning objectives**
>
> In this chapter you will learn about:
> - unrest in Britain in the early twentieth century
> - interpreting sources.

Watch out!

Sources A and B on page 65 are both primary sources. Many students make the mistake of thinking that sources that come from the time they are studying are more reliable than secondary sources written later by historians. Do not make this assumption. A secondary source based on a range of evidence collected by a historian can be just as reliable as a primary source – or even more so.

Pre-war difficulties

The Liberal government elected in 1906 introduced old age pensions, and sickness and unemployment benefits. But it was less successful in industrial relations. Between 1910 and 1914, there was a series of strikes in Britain, many of which were caused by a desire among industrial workers to control the industries in which they worked. In 1910 there were strikes by miners, cotton workers, boilermakers and railwaymen. In 1911 a national rail strike and a dockers' strike in Liverpool were both broken up by government troops. Four strikers were killed in the fighting. In 1913 three of the most powerful groups of workers in the country, the miners, the railwaymen and the transport workers, joined together to form the Triple Alliance. They agreed to help each other oppose any action by the government or employers which they believed was not in the best interests of their members.

The wave of industrial unrest which hit Britain in the years 1910–14 came to an end when war broke out. Trade union leaders agreed to 'terminate all existing trade disputes' in order to concentrate on winning the war. However, there were still unofficial strikes in parts of Britain and membership of trade unions doubled during the war. It was obvious that many of Britain's workers were unhappy with their wages and working conditions and that trouble lay ahead.

N

> **July 1910**
> Railway strike.

> **September – December 1910**
> Boilermakers' strike.

●Newcastle

> **August 1911**
> Dockers strike riot quelled by troops. Two men killed.

> **August 1911**
> Rioting during National rail strike. Two men shot dead by troops while looting shops and a train.

> **November 1910**
> Riot during miners' strike. Churchill delays army intervention. No deaths.

Liverpool●

> **May 1912**
> Dock strike. Government refuses to intervene. Strike collapses after a month.

Llanelli● ●Tonypandy

●London

> **August 1911**
> Eleven-day strike of 20,000 dockers.

0   100 miles

0   100 kilometres

Return to unrest

When the war ended, industrial unrest broke out again. Some of it came from unexpected quarters. In 1918 and 1919, the police held strikes to protest against their low wages. During the war the cost of living had almost doubled, but policemen had received only a small increase. As one striker in 1918 said 'We policemen see young van boys and slips of girls earning very much more money than we get and – well, it makes us feel sore.' It was true that, even after an increase in 1918, the police earned less than an unskilled labourer. As a result of the strikes, the government passed the Police Act of 1919, which made it illegal for the police to strike.

In the years after the war, strike action became more common and in 1921 more than 85 million working days were lost to strikes. By 1920 there were 8 million workers in the trade unions. Strike action declined after 1921 as the country went into an economic depression and workers were less prepared to take action which might threaten their jobs. Unemployment rose steadily in the traditional industries where Britain had led the world, such as textiles, shipbuilding, coalmining and steel. In the period after the war, there was less demand for these goods and unemployment rose to particularly high levels in the north-west and north-east of England, in South Wales and in Clydeside, Scotland.

In 1919, Glasgow's engineering unions called a general strike in the city in support of their demands for a 40-hour week. The government became alarmed when more than 70,000 workers demonstrated in support of the engineering workers. The government responded by sending troops and tanks to Glasgow to break up the strike.

It seemed that relations between the government and the workers were close to breaking down.

Source A	The nephew of one of the strike leaders recalled events in September 1918 when the police won an increase in their wages from the government.

Then the door of No 10 Downing Street opened and our chief negotiator, Carmichael came out. He called for silence. 'You've won' he bellowed at the sea of faces in front of him. 'This is the greatest victory for freedom and justice that has ever been won in this country.' Several years later Prime Minister Lloyd George told a policeman in the House of Commons 'This country was closer to communism that day than at any time since.'

Source B	Armed troops escorting tanks in the streets of Glasgow in January 1919.

Activities

Are you surprised by what you see in Source B?
Explain why.

Industrial unrest in the mines

> ## Learning objectives
>
> In this chapter you will learn about:
> - industrial unrest in Britain
> - considering the purpose of sources.

The greatest problems for the government were in the mining industry. During the First World War, the government had used the powers given it in the Defence of the Realm Act to take direct control of the mines. Instead of mines being under the control of a number of different owners, they were run by the government with all mines offering the same wages and conditions of employment.

The miners hoped that the government would keep control of the mines after the war and a Royal Commission (the Sankey Commission) was set up to consider how the mines should be run. It recommended that the mines should stay under government control but, despite this, the government returned them to their previous owners in March 1921. Unfortunately for the miners, this coincided with a drop in the price of coal. In 1921, prices were less than half of what they had been in 1920. The mine owners had to cut miners' wages by up to 50% and tried to lengthen the working day.

examzone
Top tip!

When asked about the purpose of a source, students often concentrate on describing what the source shows, or explaining what it says. Students who do well concentrate on 'getting behind' the surface detail to consider *why* these things have been written or drawn this way. Then they can work out the purpose of the source.

Black Friday

The Triple Alliance of 1913 had been renewed in 1919 and in the same year had proved effective in stopping the railway companies from cutting the wages of railwaymen. So the Miners' Federation asked the railwaymen and transport workers for help against the mine owners. It was agreed that there should be a joint strike on 15 April 1921. But at the last minute the railwaymen and transport workers pulled out, leaving the miners to strike on their own. Miners called this day 'Black Friday'. They continued with their strike, but by 1 July they were forced to accept the new terms and return to work. In the months that followed, dockers, railwaymen and builders also had to accept pay cuts.

Source A *A coal miner digging coal during the 1920s.*

Red Friday

In 1925 the price of coal fell once more and, again, mine owners announced a wage cut and an increase of one hour on the working day. The miners' leader, A.J. Cook, angrily announced that his men would accept 'not a penny off the pay, not a minute on the day'! This time he knew that the railwaymen and transport workers would support the miners.

Source B	*Part of an article in the* Daily Herald *on 16 April 1921. The* Daily Herald *was a newspaper paid for by the trade unions.*

Yesterday was the heaviest defeat that has befallen the Labour Movement in the history of man. It is no use trying to minimise it. It is no use trying to pretend it is other than it is. We on this paper have said throughout that if the organised workers stand together they would win. They have not stood together and they have been beaten.

The government knew it too, so on 31 July 1925 (Red Friday) the prime minister, Stanley Baldwin, announced that the government would provide a **subsidy** to keep wages at their current level for the next nine months. He also set up a commission led by Sir Herbert Samuel to find a solution to the problem in the mines.

What would happen when the subsidy ran out? Would Samuel have found an answer?

Source C	*A cartoon from the* Trade Union Unity *magazine, published in 1925. It is poking fun at the supposedly poor mine owners.*

THE SUBSIDISED MINEOWNER---POOR BEGGAR!

examzone

Build better answers

Exam question: Study Source C. What was the purpose of this representation? Use details from the cartoon and your own knowledge to explain the answer.   (8 marks)

■ **A basic answer (level 1)** makes a valid comment about purpose without using detail in the source for support OR discusses valid detail in the source without linking it to the purpose of the source.

● **A good answer (level 2)** considers the purpose of the source referring to detail in the source, own knowledge or, for a stronger answer, both.

▲ **An excellent answer (level 3)** analyses the treatment or the selection of content of the source to explain how the source was used to achieve its purpose, referring to detail in the source, own knowledge or, for a more complete level 3 answer, both.

Activities

You are a miner about to go on a protest march against the decision of your mine owner to lengthen your day and cut your wages. Draw a banner to take with you on your march. Remember that people can't read too much detail on a banner from a distance!

The General Strike

Learning objectives

In this chapter you will learn about:

- the outbreak of the strike
- the end of the strike
- considering the purpose of a source.

In March 1926, the Samuel Commission reported. It made three main recommendations:

- no increase to the working day
- wages should be cut
- mine owners to begin to modernise the pits.

On 20 April, the government subsidy ran out. Mine owners reduced wages and tried to increase hours. The miners refused to accept the increased hours, or the cut in wages. The mine owners locked them out of the mines.

The Trades Union Congress (TUC) had promised, in July 1925, to support miners if the owners tried to cut wages or raise hours again, even calling all its other members out on strike if necessary – a general strike. This was what they now threatened. Talks came to nothing. The TUC called a strike in two stages with 'first line' workers (e.g. transport services and gas and electricity workers) striking on 4 May. About 3 million workers went on strike – almost 100% in some unions.

The government had planned for this. It began to recruit special constables and volunteers to work in essential industries. It had set up emergency food depots; now it opened them and volunteers took food from the docks to fill them. It had planned for transport and emergency services; there were reduced services running by the second day of the strike.

| Source A | *A cartoon published in the* Star *newspaper on 1 June 1926. 'Stanley' refers to Stanley Baldwin, the prime minister.* |

"WHY NOT GIVE THE BACK END A SMACK, STANLEY?"

Printers, who were also first-line workers, came out on strike on 4 May. On 5 May the government led an aggressive propaganda campaign with its own newspaper, *The British Gazette*. This was full of articles about how the strike wasn't working and how volunteers were keeping the country running. The TUC's own newspaper, *The British Worker*, gave examples of how the strike was working and how much support the strikers had. It also urged the strikers not to turn to violence, even against people who were breaking the strike and volunteering to do the work of strikers.

At first the strike was successful with good humour shown on both sides. The TUC agreed that hospital workers and those who transported food should not be called out. There were even stories of strikers and police playing football matches against each other. Volunteers began to fill in the gaps left by the striking workers. So students and stockbrokers drove buses and trains, women volunteered to work on the post and more than 226,000 people volunteered as special constables to keep order.

Source B *A food convoy in Holborn, London during the strike.*

The mood turns sour

But after a few days, attitudes began to harden. Angry strikers began to clash with volunteers and some buses were set on fire. There were clashes between police and strikers in some of Britain's major cities and police made baton-charges on rioting strikers in Glasgow, Hull, Middlesbrough, Newcastle and Preston. Opposition to the strike began to grow.

The government said Britain was threatened by revolution and the Catholic Church declared the strike to be 'a sin'. There were also violent clashes between striking workers and those who chose not to go on strike.

The end of the strike

There was talk of the TUC extending the strike to cut off power supplies. Despite the fact that there was an increase in violence between strikers and volunteers, the miners wanted to see the strike extended. They asked the TUC to call out power workers and so cut off power supplies. But instead of doing so, on 12 May 1926 the TUC leaders went to 10 Downing Street for further talks with the prime minister. When they came out they announced that they had called off the strike!

This came as an enormous shock to the miners. They believed that they were being treated unfairly and hoped that the support of their fellow workers would force the government to make the mine owners back down. When the TUC called off the strike, the miners felt betrayed.

Source C *This poem was printed in the trade union newspaper, The British Worker, on 12 May 1926. In it, a worker thinking of strike-breaking explains why he cannot do so.*

Also you've promised you'd protect my skin
And save my bones and make it safe for me
To walk about and work and earn my keep
I'm not afraid for that. I know my mates
They're decent, quiet chaps, not hooligans
They wouldn't try to murder me. Not they!

But could you make them treat me as a pal
Or shield me from their cold, contemptuous eyes?
Could you restore the pride of comradeship?
Could you call back my ruined self-respect?
Give me protection from my bitter shame?
From self-contempt that drives out happiness?

Source D *An Oxford undergraduate describing the time he spent as a volunteer working in Liverpool docks.*

We set out from Oxford in a vintage Bentley and headed north. From Doncaster onwards, groups of strikers tried unsuccessfully to stop us by occasionally throwing stones or trying to puncture our tyres.

In the docks we were under the supervision of a Cambridge don, who now works as librarian at Windsor Castle.

When they returned to work, some of the old hands were surprised at the speed with which we unloaded ships but realised that it is a very different story working for a few days as an adventure, compared to regular work over many years.

Activities

1 Study Source C. Rewrite the source as one continuous piece of prose. Do you think this source would have been effective? Explain your reason for this.

2 Study Source D. In what ways is the impression given about the General Strike in this source different from that in Source C?

The TUC did have good reasons for its decision:

- It realised that the government was not prepared to be defeated. During the strike the TUC spent about £4 million and was running out of funds. The government spent about £433 million. The Organisation for the Maintenance of Supplies made sure food was distributed and gas and electricity supplies were kept on.

- The TUC was also losing the propaganda war. It saw the strike as an industrial dispute, but the government cleverly portrayed it as an attack on democracy. The TUC saw itself as representing the interests of the working man, but the government had managed to portray it as a revolutionary organisation. In actual fact, the TUC had deliberately avoided calling out workers in key areas and had worked hard to ensure picketing was peaceful. It was very worried about the clashes between police and strikers and feared they could get worse. It was also concerned about miners' demands that the strike should be extended to cut off power supplies.

- It was also true that the TUC found it hard to see how it could win the strike. The middle classes volunteered in large numbers to do the strikers' work and even seemed to be having fun!

After the strike

The General Strike was over and many employers took the opportunity to cut wages. The miners carried on with their own strike but were forced to return to work in November 1926. Wages were cut and hours increased. Mine owners took the opportunity to dismiss union leaders.

In 1927 the government passed the Trades Dispute Act. It made it illegal for workers to come out on **'sympathy strikes'** in support of other workers. It also banned civil servants from joining unions which were members of the TUC.

The General Strike had failed and the unions had been crushed. Workers saw little value in union membership and in the next few years the numbers of workers in trade unions dropped dramatically.

Exam-style question

Study Source E. What was the purpose of this representation? Use details from the cartoon and your own knowledge to explain your answer. **(8 marks)**

| Source E | A cartoon published in 1926 after the General Strike. The British lion is back at work. The caption read 'Now where were we, Miss, when that fellow interrupted us?' |

BUSINESS AS USUAL.

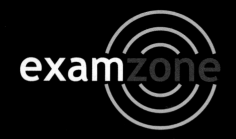

Know Zone
Unit 3A - Key Topic 4

In the Unit 3 examination, you will be required to answer five questions, applying your skills of source analysis to six sources on a topic from the Modern World Source Enquiry you have studied.

You have an hour and 15 minutes to answer these questions. Use the number of marks available for each question to help you judge how long to spend on each answer. The timings below give you some thinking time

before you start writing. Remember also to leave a few minutes at the end to check your spelling, punctuation and grammar in your answer to Question 5.

Question 1: 10 minutes   Question 4: 12 minutes
Question 2: 12 minutes   Question 5: 20 minutes
Question 3: 12 minutes

Here, we are going to look at Question 5.

examzone
Build better answers

Question 5

Tip: Question 5 will ask you to make a judgement about a hypothesis, using sources and your own knowledge. It will tell you to use a selection of sources and then say 'and any other sources you find helpful'. You must use the sources they name. However, make sure you check the other sources to see if they can help you.

In this question, it is important that you come to your own conclusion about the statement and explain how you reached this conclusion, weighing up the arguments for and against it. You can't just make something up. Consider the sources. Use your own knowledge and the captions to evaluate the sources and then use both to form a judgement about the statement.

Remember that Question 5 has 3 additional marks available for spelling, punctuation and grammar. Make sure you take extra care over the quality and accuracy of these in your answer and leave time to check it at the end.

Let's use the sources on the General Strike on pages 68–71 to answer the question:

Source B suggests that the General Strike was a serious threat to law and order in Britain. How far do you agree with this interpretation? Use your own knowledge, Sources B, C and D and any other sources you find helpful to explain your answer. (16 marks)

Student answer

The sources show there was a threat.
OR
Source B shows a tank in the street.

Comments

Both these answers can only reach level 1. The first makes a judgement without any detail from the sources or own knowledge to support it. The second answer produces some detail from the source, but doesn't explain how this relates to the question.

To reach level 2 the answer would have to say how far it agreed with the statement and then produce detail from the sources and/or own knowledge to support their view. Stronger level 2 answers use evidence from the sources and own knowledge. Let's start again.

I think it was a serious threat to law and order. Source B shows tanks on the streets. This suggests the government was worried about a threat to law and order – why else would they put tanks on the street? We know that there was some violence (Source D tells us that volunteers had stones thrown at them and strikers tried to puncture their tyres) and that volunteers in many jobs were threatened. The government had organised a lot of volunteers, but many of them didn't realise that the strike would move quickly from being quite good-humoured to violence and buses being set alight and things like that.

This answer is much better. It uses detail from two of the sources and own knowledge to support a judgement on the statement. Because it uses sources and own knowledge it is towards the top of level 2. A better answer would evaluate the evidence using two or more source and/or own knowledge. Again, using sources and own knowledge will reach the top of the level. **Answers will not reach level 3 unless supporting detail from sources is used.**

Most sources suggest there was a serious threat to law and order. Source B suggests that the government was worried about law and order being threatened – why else would they put tanks on the street? We know that they also took on 226,000 volunteer special constables. Maybe they wanted a show of strength to stop violence – but even that suggests they were taking violence seriously. Source D supports the idea that law and order was a problem – it tells us that volunteers had stones thrown at them and strikers tried to puncture their tyres. We know that buses were set alight and things like that. Source C doesn't really support it, but that is one out of all of them. Source E seems to be suggesting that the strikers broke the place up.

This is a good level 3 answer. The student makes a judgement and uses detail from several sources (including helpful detail from a source other than those listed) and own knowledge to support their view. However, they have not given a balanced answer. They haven't weighed up both sides of the argument and explained why they made the judgement they did. This would get them to level 4.

Most sources suggest there was a serious threat to law and order. Source B suggests the government was worried about law and order being threatened – why else would they put tanks on the street? We know they also took on 226,000 volunteer special constables. Maybe they wanted a show of strength to stop violence – but even that suggests they were taking violence seriously.
Source D supports the idea that law and order was a problem – it tells us that volunteers had stones thrown at them and strikers tried to puncture their tyres. We know that buses were set alight and things like that. On the other hand, Source C is saying there wouldn't be violence – but that if he broke the strike then his mates would despise him and he would despise himself for it. However, he explicitly says 'They're decent quiet chaps, not hooligans'. He's just one man, though, and writing in the trade union newspaper. So he might want to play down lawlessness. You need to wonder about the reliability of E too, it seems to support the idea that there was a threat to law and order – the office was wrecked. However, it was probably trying to brush the strike off as violent but not such a big threat it could not be stopped. I think it would be useful to have some statistic about the amount of violence and so on before deciding – but from the sources and what I have learned I think there was a real threat, probably more serious in some places than others.

This level 4 answer explores arguments for and against the view, supporting it with detail from own knowledge and several sources. It then reaches a conclusion and explains why.

Welcome to examzone

Revising for your exams can be a daunting prospect. Use this section of the book to get ideas, tips and practice to help you prepare as well as you can.

Zone In!

Have you ever become so absorbed in a task that it suddenly feels entirely natural? This is a feeling familiar to many athletes and performers: it's a feeling of being 'in the zone' that helps you focus and achieve your best.

Here are our top tips for getting in the zone with your revision.

- **Understand the exam process** and what revision you need to do. This will give you confidence but also help you to put things into proportion. Use the Planning Zone to create a revision plan.

- **Build your confidence** by using your revision time, not just to revise the information you need to know, but also to practise the skills you need for the examination. Try answering questions in timed conditions so that you're more prepared for writing answers in the exam.

- **Deal with distractions** by making a list of everything that might interfere with your revision and how you can deal with each issue. For example, revise in a room without a television, but plan breaks in your revision so that you can watch your favourite programmes.

- **Share your plan with friends and family** so that they know not to distract you when you want to revise. This will mean you can have more quality time with them when you aren't revising.

- **Keep healthy** by making sure you eat well and exercise, and by getting enough sleep. If your body is not in the right state, your mind won't be either – and staying up late to cram the night before the exam is likely to leave you too tired to do your best.

Planning Zone

The key to success in exams and revision often lies in the right planning, so that you don't leave anything until the last minute. Use these ideas to create your personal revision plan.

First, fill in the dates of your examinations. Check with your teacher when these are if you're not sure. Add in any regular commitments you have. This will help you get a realistic idea of how much time you have to revise.

Know your strengths and weaknesses and assign more time to topics you find difficult – don't be tempted to leave them until the last minute.

Create a revision 'checklist' using the Know Zone lists and use them to check your knowledge and skills.

Now fill in the timetable with sensible revision slots. Chunk your revision into smaller sections to make it more manageable and less daunting. Make sure you give yourself regular breaks and plan in different activities to provide some variety.

Keep to the timetable! Put your plan up somewhere visible so you can refer back to it and check that you are on track.

Know Zone

In this zone, you'll find checklists to help you review what you've learned and which areas you still need to work on.

Test your knowledge

Use these checklists to test your knowledge of the main areas for each topic. If you find gaps or weaknesses in your knowledge, refer back to the relevant pages of the book.

Key Topic 1

You should know about...

❏ Suffragists and suffragettes **see pages 10–11**

❏ Suffragette extremism **see pages 12–13**

❏ Opposition to the suffragettes **see pages 14–17**

❏ Rich and poor **see pages 18–19**

❏ Measures to help children **see pages 20–21**

❏ The Liberal government's social measures **see pages 22–23**

Key Topic 2

You should know about...

❏ The beginning of the war **see pages 28–29**

❏ Fighting on the Western Front **see pages 30–31**

❏ Attempts to break the stalemate on the Western Front **see pages 32–35**

❏ The failure of the British in the Battle of the Somme **see pages 36–39**

❏ The failure of Ludendorff's offensive **see pages 40–41**

Key Topic 3

You should know about...

❏ Restrictions placed on the civilian population **see pages 45–47**

❏ How the British army was recruited **see pages 48–49**

❏ Opposition to conscription **see pages 50–51**

❏ How the government dealt with food shortages **see pages 52–53**

❏ The significant part played by women in the war **see pages 54–57**

You should know about...

❏ The degree to which attitudes to women had changed **see pages 61–63**
❏ Unrest in Britain in the early twentieth century **see pages 64–65**
❏ Industrial unrest in Britain **see pages 66–67**
❏ The outbreak of the strike **see pages 68–71**
❏ The end of the strike **see pages 68–71**

Test your spelling

Remember that in question 5, the accuracy of your spelling is one element of your answer that will be assessed. Make sure you can spell the key points from each topic listed above, as well as words such as:

artillery	corps	probation
attrition	economic	propaganda
auxiliary	insurance	subsidy
barrage	martyr	rationing
budget	militant	unemployment
campaign	munitions	welfare
casualties	parliament	
censorship	pension	
conscientious objector	poverty	

Working with sources

Remember, however, that this unit is not just about recalling historical information: you need to be able to interpret and make judgments about historical sources.

As you've studied each topic, you'll have built up a range of skills for working with sources. The table below lists the main areas you should now feel confident in and shows where each is covered in the book. Refer back to those pages during your revision to check and practise your source skills.

	Key topic 1	Key topic 2	Key topic 3	Key topic 4
Making inferences from sources	pages 11 and 20		page 47	page 63
Considering the purpose of a source	page 17	page 37	page 49	page 67
Explaining causation using a source and own knowledge	page 19	page 31	pages 53 and 57	
Evaluating the reliability of sources	page 13	pages 29 and 35		
Evaluating a hypothesis		page 39		

Life on the Western Front

Answer All Questions

This question paper is about life on the Western Front.

Look carefully at the background information and Sources A–F and then answer Questions 1–5.

Question 1
Study Source A.

What can you learn from Source A about life on the Western Front? (6)

Question 2
Study Source B and use your own knowledge.

What was the purpose of this representation? Use details from the film still and your own knowledge to explain your answer. (8)

Question 3
Study Source B and use your own knowledge.

Use Source B and your own knowledge to explain why some soldiers wrote letters home like this. (10)

Question 4
Study Sources D and E and use your own knowledge.

How reliable are Sources D and E as evidence of the attitudes of soldiers on the Western Front?
Explain your answer, using Sources D and E and your own knowledge. (10)

Question 5
Study Sources A, E and F and use your own knowledge.

Spelling, punctuation and grammar will be assessed in this question.

Source E suggests that conditions on the Western Front were appalling. How far do you agree with this interpretation? Use your own knowledge, Sources A, E and F and any other sources you find helpful to explain your answer.

3 additional marks for spelling, punctuation and grammar. (16)

Background information

In 1914 Germany invaded Belgium and Britain sent the BEF to try to stop the German forces entering France. It was unable to do so and in September German troops fought against the French and British at the Battle of the Marne. This battle stopped the German advance, but it did not end the war.

Instead both sides dug in and the 'Western Front' became the main theatre of war for the next four years.

What was it like to fight on the Western Front?

Source A   A soldier remembers his first sight of death in the trenches.

> The dead man lay on the earth. Never before had I seen a man who had just been killed. His face and body were terribly gashed and the smell of blood, mixed with the fumes of the shell, made me sick. Only a great effort stopped my legs giving way and the voice seemed to whisper in my ear 'Why should you be next'?

Source B   British troops leaving the trenches in a scene from the government film *The Battle of the Somme.*

Source C   A description of the trench scene by a soldier in 1917.

> It is noon now and some of us are blowing on hot tea to cool it, or eating a hot stew of meat and potatoes out of dixie cans. The day is fine and other men are basking like cats on little sunny shelves and bunks sculptured out of the trench walls. One little knot of men are bending over a comic paper.

Source D   A soldier describes life in the trenches in 1916. The Saxons were from the part of Germany called Saxony.

> It's the Saxons that's across the road. They are quiet fellows, the Saxons and they don't want to fight any more than we do. So there's a kind of understanding between us. You don't fire at us and we won't fire at you.

Source E   A soldier describes how conditions in the trenches affected him in September 1916.

> I was wet to the skin, no overcoat, no water sheet. I had about 3 inches of clay clinging to my clothes and it was cold. Do you know what I did? I sat down in the mud and I cried. I do not think I have cried like that since I was a baby.

Source F   An advertising poster from the First World War.

Don't Panic Zone

As the day of the exam gets closer, many students tend to go into panic mode, either working long hours without really giving their brain a chance to absorb information, or giving up and staring blankly at the wall.

Look over your revision notes and go through the checklists to remind yourself of the main areas you need to know about. Don't try to cram in too much new information at the last minute and don't stay up late revising – you'll do better if you get a good night's sleep.

Exam Zone

What to expect in the exam paper

You will have 1 hour and 15 minutes in the examination. There will be five questions and you should answer all of these. There will be between six and eight sources in a separate source booklet; some of these will be written and some illustrations.

Question 1 is an inference question worth 6 marks. It will ask what a source is suggesting, usually phrased as 'What can you learn from Source X?' You should spend about 10 minutes on this question. For an example, see page 24.

Question 2 is a source analysis question worth 8 marks. It will ask you about the purpose of the source, for example 'Why was the source produced?' or 'Why was this photograph used?' You should spend about 12 minutes on this question. 'You must refer to the source and your own knowledge in this question.' For an example, see page 25.

Question 3 is worth 10 marks and involves explaining causation using a source and your own knowledge. The question will usually be in the form 'Use Source A and your own knowledge to explain why ...' **You cannot reach the highest level without using detail from your own knowledge**. You should spend about 12 minutes on this question. For an example, see pages 42–43.

Question 4 is worth 10 marks and asks you to evaluate the reliability of two sources, using the sources and your own knowledge. It is important to evaluate both sources and use supporting detail from your own knowledge. It is usually phrased as 'How reliable are Sources A and B as evidence of ...?' You should spend about 12 minutes on this question. For an example, see pages 58–59.

Question 5 is a judgement question worth 16 marks. It will start with a statement and then ask 'How far do you agree with this view? Use your own knowledge, Sources A, D and F and any other sources you find useful to explain your answer.' Remember there are up to 3 additional marks for spelling, punctuation and grammar for your answer to this question. You should spend about 20 minutes on this question. For an example, see pages 72–73.

Meet the exam paper

This diagram shows the front cover of the exam paper. These instructions, information and advice will always appear on the front of the paper. It is worth reading it carefully now. Check you understand it and ask your teacher about anything you are not sure of.

Print your surname here, and your other names afterwards. This is an additional safeguard to ensure that the exam board awards the marks to the right candidate.

Here you fill in the school's exam number.

The Unit 3 exam lasts 1 hour 15 minutes. Plan your time accordingly.

Make sure that you answer all questions.

Remember to check your spelling, punctuation and grammar when you see this.

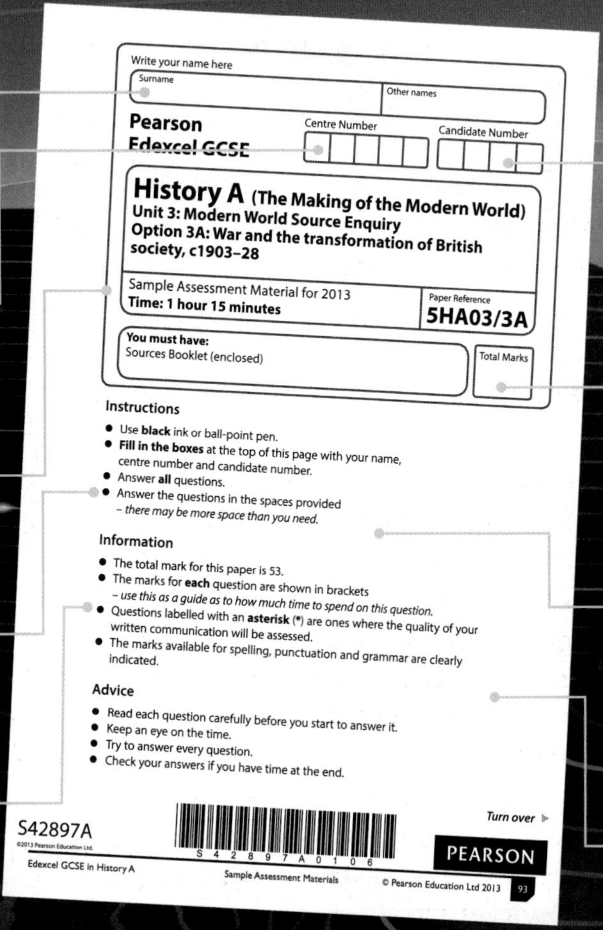

Write your name here
Surname | Other names

Pearson Edexcel GCSE
Centre Number | Candidate Number

History A (The Making of the Modern World)
Unit 3: Modern World Source Enquiry
Option 3A: War and the transformation of British society, c1903–28

Sample Assessment Material for 2013
Time: 1 hour 15 minutes

Paper Reference
5HA03/3A

You must have:
Sources Booklet (enclosed)

Total Marks

Instructions

- Use **black** ink or ball-point pen.
- **Fill in the boxes** at the top of this page with your name, centre number and candidate number.
- Answer **all** questions.
- Answer the questions in the spaces provided – *there may be more space than you need.*

Information

- The total mark for this paper is 53.
- The marks for **each** question are shown in brackets – *use this as a guide as to how much time to spend on this question.*
- Questions labelled with an **asterisk** (*) are ones where the quality of your written communication will be assessed.
- The marks available for spelling, punctuation and grammar are clearly indicated.

Advice

- Read each question carefully before you start to answer it.
- Keep an eye on the time.
- Try to answer every question.
- Check your answers if you have time at the end.

Turn over

S42897A
©2013 Pearson Education Ltd.

PEARSON

Edexcel GCSE in History A | Sample Assessment Materials | © Pearson Education Ltd 2013 | 93

Here you fill in your personal exam number. Take care to write it accurately.

In this box, the examiner will write the total marks you have achieved in the exam paper.

Don't feel that you have to fill the answer space provided. Everybody's handwriting varies, so a long answer from you may take up as much space as a short answer from someone else.

Remember that in Question 5 the quality of your written communication will be assessed. Take time to check your spelling, punctuation and grammar and to make sure that you have expressed yourself clearly.

Answer ALL questions.

Look carefully at Sources A to F in the Sources Booklet and then answer Questions 1 to 5 which follow.

1 Study Source A.

What can you learn from Source A about the recruitment of women during the First World War?

(6)

_____

_____

_____

_____

_____

_____

_____

_____

_____

_____

_____

_____

_____

_____

_____

The live question paper will contain one further page of lines.

(Total for Question 1 = 6 marks)

In Unit 3 you need to answer all five questions on the paper.

Each question will tell you which source or sources you need to read in the sources booklet.

The number of marks available for each question is given on the right.

Read the detail about the provenance and date of each source carefully before studying the source.

Historical Enquiry: The role of women

Source A: An Appeal for Land Workers made by *The Daily News and Leader*, a national newspaper, 15 February 1916.

> The country has raised an army, still growing, of 250,000 women for munitions factories. There now remains the problem of mobilising another army of 400,000 women for work on the land. This is the most difficult problem of all. Work on the land is not popular among those women most able to do it. No woman can be expected to enjoy milking cows at four a.m. on a winter morning, or spreading manure, or cleaning a pigsty. Much of the most necessary work is hard and unpleasant and by no means well paid. That is why the appeal is aimed at the patriotism of women.

Source B: This painting called *For King and Country* is a representation of women working in a munitions factory. It was painted in 1916 by an official government war artist.

Zone Out

This section provides answers to the most common questions students have about what happens after they complete their exams. For more information, visit www.examzone.co.uk.

When will my results be published?

Results for GCSE examinations are issued on the third Thursday in August.

Can I get my results online?

Visit www.resultsplusdirect.co.uk, where you will find detailed student results information including the 'Edexcel Gradeometer' which demonstrates how close you were to the nearest grade boundary.

I haven't done as well as I expected. What can I do now?

First of all, talk to your teacher. After all the teaching that you have had, and the tests and internal examinations you have done, he/she is the person who best knows what grade you are capable of achieving. Take your results slip to your subject teacher, and go through the information on it in detail. If you both think that there is something wrong with the result, the school or college can apply to see your completed examination paper and then, if necessary, ask for a re-mark immediately.

Can I have a re-mark of my examination paper?

Yes, this is possible, but remember only your school or college can apply for a re-mark, not you or your parents/carers. First of all you should consider carefully whether or not to ask your school or college to make a request for a re-mark. It is worth knowing that very few re-marks result in a change to a grade, simply because a re-mark request has shown that the original marking was accurate. Check the closing date for re-marking requests with your Examinations Officer.

Bear in mind that there is no guarantee that your grades will go up if your papers are re-marked. The original mark can be confirmed or lowered, as well as raised, as a result of a re-mark.

Glossary

Term	Definition
absolutist	A conscientious objector who refused to play any role in the war.
adultery	Being unfaithful to one's husband or wife.
attrition	A policy of waging war by wearing down the enemy's resources.
blockade	Setting up a barrier to stop goods reaching their destination.
borstals	Residential homes for children too young to go to prison.
breakthrough	To pierce the enemy defences and push through their trench system.
casualties	Soldiers killed, wounded or captured in battle.
casual work	Non-permanent work with a high risk of unemployment.
censor	To control or alter information. Censorship involved controlling the information people received.
commuted	Changed to or lessened. Death sentences could be commuted to life imprisonment.
convoy	A collection of merchant ships sailing together under protection from warships.
creeping barrage	Artillery fire moving slowly forward in front of advancing soldiers.
fervour	Enthusiasm or excitement. Patriotic fervour was strong support for one's country.
heckle	To jeer at or abuse a speaker at a meeting.
laid off	What happened to casual workers when there was no more work.
landslide	An overwhelming victory.
martyr	Someone prepared to die for a cause.
merchant shipping	Ships bringing goods to or from overseas markets.
militant	Prepared to take action or strong measures.
non-combatant	Not involved with fighting. Some conscientious objectors did non-combatant duties at the front.
poverty line	The minimum standard of living a human should have.

probation	A method of dealing with criminals (particularly young people) which puts them under the care of a probation officer, who monitors their behaviour.
rationing	Controlling supplies by limiting the amount people can have.
stalemate	The situation on the Western Front when neither side could break through the enemy's defences.
subsidy	A sum of money provided (by the government) to help in times of need.
suffrage	The right to vote.
suffragettes	Women who were prepared to take militant action to get the vote.
suffragist	Women who wanted to achieve the vote through peaceful campaigning.
sympathy strikes	A form of strike by a group of workers to support their colleagues working in other industries.
tribunal	An organisation set up to hear, for example, appeals by conscientious objectors against being called up.
welfare state	A system where the state believes in looking after those citizens who cannot look after themselves.
workhouse	An institution which provided basic shelter and work for people who could not support themselves.

Published by Pearson Education Limited, Edinburgh Gate, Harlow, Essex, CM20 2JE.

www.pearsonschoolsandfecolleges.co.uk

Copies of official specifications for all Edexcel qualifications may be found on the Edexcel website: www.edexcel.com

Text © Pearson Education Limited 2013
Typeset by HL Studios, Witney, Oxford
Illustrated by Peter Bull Studio
Cover photo/illustration © Front: **Getty Images:** Hulton Archive

The rights of Jane Shuter and Nigel Kelly to be identified as authors of this work have been asserted by them in accordance with the Copyright, Designs and Patents Act 1988.

First published 2013

16 15 14 13
10 9 8 7 6 5 4 3 2 1

British Library Cataloguing in Publication Data
A catalogue record for this book is available from the British Library

ISBN 978 1 446 92409 9

Printed in Italy by Lego S.p.A

Acknowledgements
The author and publisher would like to thank the following individuals and organisations for permission to reproduce photographs:

(Key: b-bottom; c-centre; l-left; r-right; t-top)

6 John Frost Newspapers. 7 akg-images Ltd: NordicPhotos. **8 Corbis:** Hulton-Deutsch Collection. **9 Corbis:** Fine Art Photographic Library.
10 akg-images Ltd: British Library. **11 Corbis:** Hulton-Deutsch Collection. **12 Corbis:** Bettmann. **13 Mary Evans Picture Library. 14 Mary Evans Picture Library. 15 Bridgeman Art Library Ltd:** The Stapleton Collection. **16 Getty Images:** English School. **17 Bridgeman Art Library Ltd:** English School. **18 Corbis:** Hulton-Deutsch Collection. **19 Corbis:** Hulton-Deutsch Collection. **21 Bridgeman Art Library Ltd:** Museum of London/John Galt (r). **Getty Images:** Fox Photos (l). **22 Mary Evans Picture Library. 23 The Art Archive:** John Meek. **26 Corbis:** Bettmann. **27 Corbis:** Hulton-Deutsch Collection. **29 Corbis:** Bettmann. **30 Getty Images:** Popperfoto/Paul Popper. **31 Bridgeman Art Library Ltd:** English School. **32 Getty Images:** General Photographic Agency. **33 Imperial War Museum:** Sargent, John Singer RA. **34 Corbis:** Bettmann. **35 Getty Images:** Topical Press Agency. **36 Alamy Images:** Seapix. **37 Getty Images:** Popperfoto/Paul Popper. **38 Imperial War Museum:** Geoffrey Malins. **40 Getty Images:** General Photographic Agency (b). **41 Alamy Images:** Ian Nellist. **44 Corbis:** Hulton-Deutsch Collection. **46 Mitchell Library:** Glasgow City Archives. **48 Bridgeman Art Library Ltd:** The Stapleton Collection. **49 Corbis:** Hulton-Deutsch Collection. **51 Bridgeman Art Library Ltd:** English School. **Getty Images:** Hulton Archive (t). **Imperial War Museum:** Frank Holland (b). **54 Imperial War Museum:** Skinner, Edward F. **55 Getty Images:** Topical Press Agency. **57 Corbis:** Hulton-Deutsch Collection. **60 Corbis:** Hulton-Deutsch Collection. **61 Corbis:** Hulton-Deutsch Collection. **62 Mirrorpix:** W. K. Haselden, Daily Mirror, 1 Mar 1924, British Cartoon Archive, University of Kent, www.cartoons.ac.uk. **65 Herald & Times Glasgow. 66 Getty Images:** Sasha. **67 TUC Library Collections:** London Metropolitan University. **68 Solo Syndication:** Associated Newspapers Ltd, David Low, The Star, 1 Jun 1926, British Cartoon Archive, University of Kent, www.cartoons.ac.uk. **69 Corbis:** Hulton-Deutsch Collection. **71 Express Syndication:** Sidney 'George' Strube. **78 Getty Images:** Popperfoto/Paul Popper. **79 Bridgeman Art Library Ltd:** Dadd, Frank (1851-1929)/Private Collection/Topham Picturepoint. **82 Mary Evans Picture Library:** R Caton Woodville

We are grateful to the following for permission to reproduce copyright material:

Source A: page 12 from Describing an attack on a London magistrate by suffragettes in Margate., *The Standard*, 4 June 1913; Source C, page 13 from Article about the death of Emily Davison, The Times, 5 June 1913; Source A, page 20 from *The Yorkshire Post*, 1903; Source A, page 28 from *The First World War*, 1969 ISBN-13: 978-0435310431, Heinemann (Nigel Kelly 1969), Pearson Education; Source B, page 37 after *Forgotten Voices of the Somme: The Most Devastating Battle of the Great War in the Words of Those Who Survived* ISBN-13: 978-0091926281 Page 135 Ebury Press (Joshua Levine) Original interview sourced from Imperial War Museum Sound Archive Ref: 16458; Source C, page 41 from *The First Day on the Somme: 1 July 1916* ISBN-13: 978-0140171341 Page 300 Penguin History (Martin Middlebrook) 29 Jun 2006, with permission from Penguin Books Ltd; Source D, page 46 from Article complaining about the censorship imposed by DORA, *The Nation Magazine*, May 1916, The Nation Magazine; Source C, page 49 from *A Duration Man: A Staffordshire Soldier in the Great War – Ypres, the Somme and Passchendaele and Italy* ISBN-13: 978-1897949610, Churnet Valley Books (Austin J Heraty) Dec 1999; Source C, page 53 from *The Observer*, 8 April 1917; Source C, page 70 from From 'Meditations of a Trade Unionist on Reading Mr Baldwin's Guarantees to Strike- Breakers' The British Worker No 3 (Manchester edition) TUC Library Collections 12 May 1926, TRADES UNION CONGRESS

Every effort has been made to contact copyright holders of material reproduced in this book. Any omissions will be rectified in subsequent printings if notice is given to the publishers.

A note from the publisher
In order to ensure that this student book offers high-quality support for the associated Edexcel qualification, it has been through a review process by the awarding organisation to confirm that it fully covers the teaching and learning content of the specification or part of a specification at which it is aimed, and demonstrates an appropriate balance between the development of subject skills, knowledge and understanding, in addition to preparation for assessment.

While the publishers have made every attempt to ensure that advice on the qualification and its assessment is accurate, the official specification and associated assessment guidance materials are the only authoritative source of information and should always be referred to for definitive guidance.

Edexcel examiners have not contributed to any updated sections in this resource relevant to examination papers for which they have responsibility.

No material from an endorsed student book will be used verbatim in any assessment set by Edexcel.

Endorsement of a student book does not mean that the student book is required to achieve this Edexcel qualification, nor does it mean that it is the only suitable material available to support the qualification, and any resource lists produced by the awarding organisation shall include this and other appropriate resources.